The U

OUTI

BOOK

Written by David Watkins, Meike Dalal, Bridget Gibbs
and Rosamund Kidman Cox

Illustrated by Jonathan Langley and Malcolm English
with additional artwork by Andy Martin, Sally Burrough
and Michael Roffe

Photography by Ken Pilsbury

Edited by Bridget Gibbs

Designed by Sally Burrough

Design assistant Niki Overy

Special consultants
Peter C. Nicholls, author and lecturer in outdoor
education; Chairman, Physical Activities Panel, the
Duke of Edinburgh's Award in Australia.
Brian Porteous, Professional Officer of the British
Orienteering Federation.
Beatrice Tannant, SRN, RSCN, SCM, RN Canada.

We would like to thank the following organizations for their help
in producing this book:
The St. John Ambulance Association in Britain and Australia
The Royal Life Saving Society
The London Fire Brigade

First published in 1979 by Usborne Publishing
Ltd., 20 Garrick Street, London WC2E 9BJ,
England.

Copyright © 1979 Usborne Publishing Ltd.

Published in Canada by Hayes Publishing Ltd.,
Burlington, Ontario.

Printed in England by Waterlow (Dunstable) L

The material in this book is also available as three
separate books: Exploring and Finding the Way,
Living Outdoors, and First Aid and Emergencies,
in the Outdoor Guides series, published by
Usborne Publishing Limited.

Contents

Starting to explore

The first section of this book (up to page 61) tells you how to start exploring and finding the way, using a map and a compass. It also tells you all the things you need to know before you set off hiking or cycling – what food to take, what to wear, how to tell what the weather will be like, how to plan your route, and so on. There is also advice on what to do if things go wrong – if you get lost, or if you have a puncture, for example. When you have practised the basic skills, exploring the area nearest your home, you will be better prepared to explore further afield. It is safer and more fun to do this with friends, rather than alone.

Take a camera with you if you have one. It is one good way to record what you see.

Notepad and pencils are useful for jotting down any questions and making sketches.

Always take a map of the area with you. Study it thoroughly before you set out.

Plan your route

If you know which places you want to visit, you can mark them on a map of the area and then plan the best route to see them. You need not stick rigidly to your plan if you see something else interesting, but it is a good way to start.

Another way to explore is to climb up to a high place, such as the top of a hill or tower, where you can get a good view. Make a note of anything interesting you see and then go and visit it.

Try wandering around an area at random. If you see anything that particularly interests you, follow it up. Always take a map and compass with you, and be sure you know how to use them.

Choose a special subject

A good idea is to decide on a special subject and then explore by searching for whatever you have chosen. This way you will have to ask lots of people for directions, so you will learn your way around a new place. Choose things like windows, flowers, or specialist shops, and look for as many different kinds as possible.

Use your senses

When you are out, keep your eyes open for the unexpected at all times. Listen to what's going on around you and notice if there are any distinctive smells. Touch things to see what they feel like.

Exploring towns

First, find a map of the town. You may be able to get one free from an estate agent, tourist office or information centre. Look at guide books and go to the local library to find out about places to visit. Try to find out why the town grew up there, how old it is and what industry it has.

Why is the town there?

Has the town grown up at the crossing point of two roads?

Is it a market town and what kind of things are sold?

Is the town by a river, at the point where a bridge crosses it?

The style of building will give you an idea of how old the town is.

Look for details like carving and wall plaques which will help you.

Road names often tell a lot about a town's past. People, events, descriptions of places and trades are common.

A big railway station will tell you that the town is an important centre of communications or has some major industry.

Use local museums to find out about history and wildlife, and any famous people who lived in the area.

Look for docks, work-shops and warehouses to give you some idea of the town's industries.

Find out more about industry, past and present, by looking around at factories, mills and machinery.

If there is a river or a canal, follow it to see where it goes. Look for features such as bridges and locks.

Many larger towns have zoos which are well worth a visit. Notice that zoos are always situated near built-up areas or major roads to attract as many people as possible.

Parks, botanical gardens and even waste ground are all interesting places to look around. You will be surprised at how many different plants you find growing in towns.

7

Exploring the countryside

Farms

If you explore the countryside, you are likely to travel over farmland. Look at the buildings and the variety of machinery being used. Notice which crops are growing and the type of soil, and whether the farmer keeps cows or other animals.

Buildings

Even in the countryside you will come across an interesting variety of buildings. Look out for churches, windmills, watermills, country houses, castles, monuments etc. Does the building tell you anything about the history of the area?

Historical sites

In many areas there are historical sites to explore. You may even be able to find an archaeological dig which you can take part in.

Structures

You could also look out for structures such as road bridges, aquaducts, dams, observatories and radio telescopes.

Things to look for in the countryside

Find out about events such as horse shows and sports meetings.

The tourist office, local library or newspapers will have

details of carnivals, fetes, fairs and other events in their area.

Go insect-watching or birdwatching. Take photographs, but don't pick flowers or take eggs from birds' nests.

Look out for areas with underground caves. Go on a guided tour and see the rock formations.

Find out about the history of local industries, such as quarries. What rocks are found in the area?

Geyser

Natural features such as springs, waterfalls, geysers, lakes and canyons are often impressive and well worth a visit. They will be shown on a map of the area, so you can plan your route to include them. If you keep your eyes open, you may see other unexpected features of equal interest, such as unusual rock formations.

Respecting the countryside

Before you go exploring the countryside, read through and memorize the points on these pages. It is important to respect all wild animals and plants so that you do not spoil the countryside for other people.

DO'S . . .

. . . & DON'TS

Great Britain

Elsewhere

DO WALK TOWARDS ONCOMING TRAFFIC WHEN YOU ARE WALKING ON ROADS (i.e. ON THE RIGHT IN BRITAIN)

DON'T LEAVE RUBBISH LYING AROUND — TAKE IT HOME WITH YOU

DO WEAR LIGHT-COLOURED CLOTHES, SO YOU CAN BE SEEN

DON'T PULL UP FLOWERS OR PLANTS – IT IS DESTRUCTIVE AND IS ILLEGAL IN SOME PLACES

DO'S ...	... & DON'TS

DO BE WARY OF ANIMALS—FIND OUT ABOUT ANY THAT MAY BE DANGEROUS IN YOUR AREA

DON'T CHASE ANIMALS—THEY MAY TURN ON YOU OR INJURE THEMSELVES

DO CLOSE GATES BEHIND YOU TO PREVENT ANIMALS ESCAPING

DON'T FORCE YOUR WAY THROUGH FENCES, WALLS OR HEDGES – IF YOU DAMAGE THEM, ANIMALS MAY ESCAPE

DO WALK AROUND FIELDS IF THERE IS NO FOOTPATH, OTHERWISE YOU MAY DAMAGE CROPS

DON'T THROW THINGS INTO PONDS, STREAMS OR TROUGHS WHERE ANIMALS ARE LIKELY TO DRINK

DO BE CAREFUL WITH FIRE – IT CAN EASILY GET OUT OF CONTROL

DON'T MAKE TOO MUCH NOISE, OR PLAY RADIOS OR CASSETTE PLAYERS. IT WILL DISTURB OTHER PEOPLE AND ANIMALS

DO KEEP YOUR DOG ON A LEAD SO THAT IT DOESN'T RUN AROUND AND FRIGHTEN ANIMALS

11

Walking gear

Before you set out exploring, check that you are properly equipped. What you need to take depends on the length of trip planned, the climate and your hobbies. These pages show the main items you will need for a day trip.

Clothes

Hat *Keeps you warm if it's cold, and gives protection against the sun if it's hot, so you don't suffer sunstroke.*

Waterproof jacket with hood *for protection from rain and wind. It is useful to have a jacket that packs away into a pocket.*

Jumper *Always take one with you, even in hot climates, as nights can get quite cold. If you plan to be on high ground, remember that the temperature drops as you go higher up. In cool climates you will need two jumpers.*

Shorts *or* **jeans** *Shorts are more comfortable in hot weather, except in forest or bush. But wear jeans if you get sunburnt easily.*

Shoes *Thick-soled walking shoes or boots are best in the country. Always break in a new pair before using them for long walks.*

Socks *Two pairs of thick woollen socks are best. Long ones protect your legs in rough undergrowth and can be rolled down if it's hot.*

Walking boots

Feet

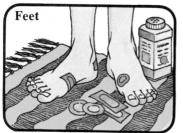

Look after your feet carefully. Wash them thoroughly every day, dry well and use foot powder generously. Put plasters on sore spots before blisters develop.

Pack

You will need a light, comfortable pack like this one. Do not make the mistake of getting a big pack for day hikes; the larger the pack, the more you will take.

Food and drink

Dehydrated food

Solid fuel stove

Take sandwiches and fresh fruit to eat at midday. Nuts, dried fruit and chocolate can be nibbled between meals for extra energy.

In cold weather, you may want a hot midday meal. Take hot food in a vacuum flask, or try dehydrated food, which is light to carry and can be heated on a lightweight stove, but needs water for mixing (see page 60).

Take a cold fruit drink, not the fizzy type, in a plastic bottle, or have a hot drink in a vacuum flask.

Other things to take with you

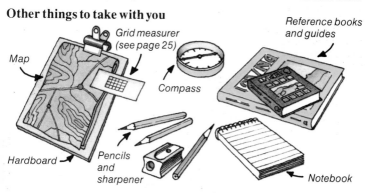

Map

Grid measurer (see page 25)

Compass

Reference books and guides

Hardboard

Pencils and sharpener

Notebook

Cycling

If you are going to use your bicycle for exploring the countryside, it is best to start by making several short journeys over different types of ground. Make a note of how far you can cycle comfortably each time. You can then use this information to help you plan cycle trips.

Keep to tracks or minor roads with few cars.

Go for weekend trips before you attempt longer tours, so that you find out what equipment you really need to take and what can be left behind, keeping your load as light as possible. Make sure you pack your gear into special bags like those shown opposite, so that you can cycle safely.

The parts of a bicycle

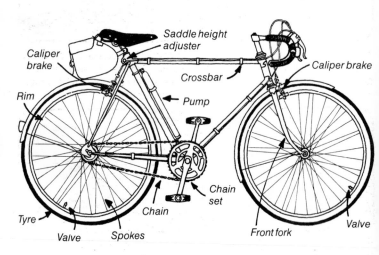

Saddle height adjuster

Caliper brake

Caliper brake

Crossbar

Rim

Pump

Tyre

Valve

Chain set

Chain

Valve

Spokes

Front fork

Get to know the parts of your bicycle, then use pages 18 and 19 to learn how to mend a puncture, a broken chain and faulty brakes.

Wrong

Right

Never carry things on your back when cycling. It is uncomfortable and dangerous, affecting your ability to balance and steer. If you have a lot to carry, use waterproof bags called "panniers" strapped to special frames fixed over the wheels. It is important to spread the load back and front to balance the bicycle.

A basket like this on the front of the bicycle is useful for carrying a map and compass, food, drink, and a waterproof jacket.

A saddle bag can be used instead of or as well as a basket, and will keep things dry if it rains. It straps onto the saddle.

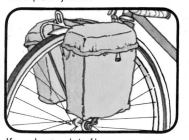

If you have a lot of heavy gear on the back of the bike, use front panniers, strapped to a frame like this, to balance it up.

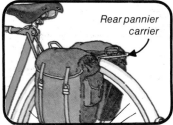

Rear pannier carrier

Back panniers are larger than front ones, and are good for bulky things like your tent. Remember to keep wet and dry things separate.

Bicycle safety

Take care when riding a loaded bicycle. It will go faster than usual downhill and take longer to brake.

Make sure the saddle is adjusted so that you can touch the ground with the balls of your feet.

Ride in single file and signal clearly well before you turn. Glance behind frequently to check on the traffic.

Wear a fluorescent waistcoat or patches so that motorists can see you clearly.

Make sure your bicycle has front and rear lights. Put them on as soon as daylight starts to fade, and whenever bad weather makes it difficult for cars to see you.

Make the width of your cycle clear by fixing a wooden bar like this with reflectors to your rear carrier. Or you can buy reflector tape to fix onto rear panniers or mudguard.

Cycle kit

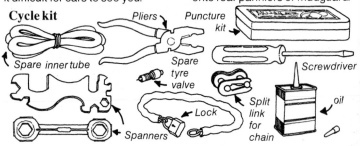

Spare inner tube — Pliers — Puncture kit — Spare tyre valve — Screwdriver — Split link for chain — oil — Lock — Spanners

Maintenance and repairs

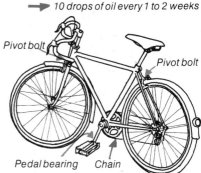

→ 1-2 drops of oil every 3 to 6 weeks
→ 10 drops of oil every 1 to 2 weeks

Check over your bicycle at least once a week for signs of wear. The points indicated in the illustration should be oiled with a light machine oil as specified. You should also oil hub gears regularly; use about half a teaspoon of oil once a month.

Check to see that all parts move freely but with as little side play as possible. If any part wobbles, tighten the nut.

Pivot bolt

Pivot bolt

Pedal bearing   *Chain*

Nuts and bolts

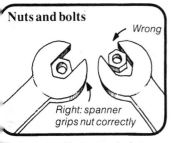

Wrong

Right: spanner grips nut correctly

Test nuts and bolts regularly to see if any have worked loose. When you tighten a nut, always make sure you use the right size spanner, and that you grip the nut correctly.

Tyres

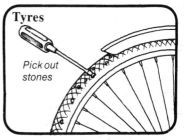

Pick out stones

Keep tyres pumped up hard and replace them as soon as they look worn. Pick out any stones lodged in them with a screwdriver. Wobbly wheels or broken spokes are best adjusted in a bicycle shop.

Lights

Make sure your lights work properly. If they run on batteries rather than dynamo, replace the battery as soon as it gets weak.

Cleaning

Clean your bicycle regularly. Wipe round wheel rims with a clean, dry cloth to keep brakes working well.

More bicycle repairs

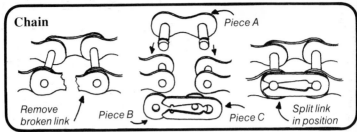

Chain

Remove broken link   Piece B   Piece C   Piece A   Split link in position

If your bicycle chain breaks, you can mend it with a split link. First remove the broken link. Then push piece A of the split link through the chain so that it links the two ends. Put piece B over the ends of piece

A sticking through the chain, then use a screwdriver to clip piece C on top to hold the link in position. The rounded end of piece C should point in the direction the chain moves.

Brakes

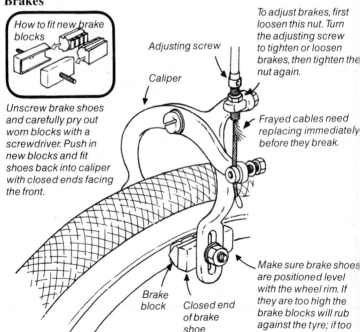

How to fit new brake blocks

Adjusting screw

Caliper

To adjust brakes, first loosen this nut. Turn the adjusting screw to tighten or loosen brakes, then tighten the nut again.

Unscrew brake shoes and carefully pry out worn blocks with a screwdriver. Push in new blocks and fit shoes back into caliper with closed ends facing the front.

Frayed cables need replacing immediately before they break.

Brake block

Closed end of brake shoe

Make sure brake shoes are positioned level with the wheel rim. If they are too high the brake blocks will rub against the tyre; if too low, the brakes will not work well.

Mending a puncture

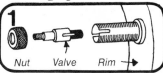

Nut Valve Rim →

If you think you have a puncture, first check the valve to make sure air is not leaking from it, by putting spit on the end of it.

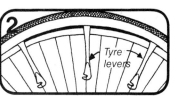

Tyre levers

If the valve is not the source of the leak, remove the wheel from the bicycle and lever the tyre off. Be careful not to pinch the inner tube.

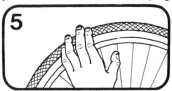

Remove the inner tube and pump some air into it. Then hold it in a bowl of water until you see bubbles coming from it. Or, hold the tube to your ear and listen for air escaping.

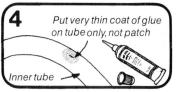

Put very thin coat of glue on tube only, not patch

Inner tube →

Dry the tube. Choose a patch from your repair kit big enough to cover the hole and the surrounding area. Apply glue to tube and leave until tacky before sticking patch down.

Before you put the tube back in the tyre, run your fingers over both the inside and outside of the tyre to make sure that whatever caused the puncture is not still there.

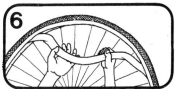

To replace the tube, put the valve part way through the hole in the rim, pump a little air in, and then feed it carefully under the tyre.

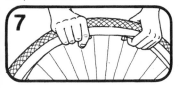

Push the tyre over the rim and back into position, kneeding it into place with your hands. Do not use tyre levers for doing this.

Bicycle frame (rear view) Wheel

Pump up the tyre fully and replace the wheel on the bicycle. Make sure the wheel is positioned in the centre of the frame.

Getting ready

Whether you are planning to go out just for a day, or for a week or more, it will need some preparation. If you are not intending to explore locally, you will need to decide how you are going to get to your chosen area, and then find out about coach or train times if necessary.

Learn to map read. Pages 22 to 31 tell you about maps and map reading. Buy a relief map of the area in which you live (an Ordnance Survey map) and practise map reading so that you can visualize landscapes and symbols.

When you feel confident about map reading, buy a compass and learn how to use it (see pages 32 to 39). Practise using the map and compass together. They are vital equipment for anyone interested in walking or cycling.

The amount of equipment you will need depends on how long you are going for. A shoulder bag or small back pack should be big enough for a day hike but you will need a framed rucksack for longer holidays.

If you are going for more than a day, you will need to camp or to stay at youth hostels. If you intend camping, get experience by camping out overnight a few times in your own or a friend's garden, and then by trying several weekend camps near home.

Buy or borrow a touring guide book to find out where there are youth hostels or camp sites in the area you are going to visit.

Find out about typical weather conditions there. Holiday brochures have notes on weather, or try writing to the local chamber of commerce for information.

If you have a camera or can borrow one, it is worth finding room in your pack for it so that you will be able to make an illustrated record of your trip. Experiment with the camera at home until you can get good shots all the time. Blurred photographs or ones that show only part of the intended subject will not be much use.

Maps

Maps are made for all kinds of purposes. The type you need for walking and cycling are relief or topographical maps, known as Ordnance Survey maps in Britain. These maps help you to understand what an area is like before you have even been there. You can see whether the land is flat or hilly, and where there are towns, rivers, parks, forests or other features.

A map is a diagrammatic bird's-eye view of the ground. Some maps are made from aerial photographs, which look rather like this.

What do relief maps show?

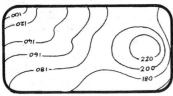

Relief maps show the shape of the land by means of contour lines like these. See pages 29 to 31 for more about contours.

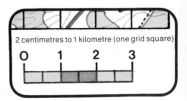

2 centimetres to 1 kilometre (one grid square)

Maps are drawn to scale, so they show the distance between places and the size of things like towns. Scale is explained on page 26.

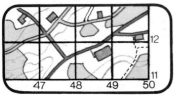

Maps show the positions of places. Using the numbered grid, you can tell someone exactly where something is. See pages 24 and 25.

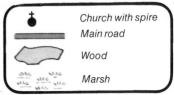

Church with spire
Main road
Wood
Marsh

Features are shown by symbols like these. Symbols vary from country to country, but are always explained in a key on the map.

Different types of map

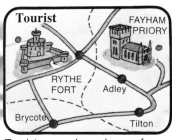

Tourist

Tourist maps show places of interest such as stately homes, castles, monuments and zoos, and the main roads for getting there.

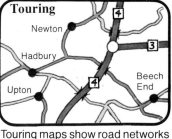

Touring

Touring maps show road networks and towns. They are intended for motorists who are travelling long distances.

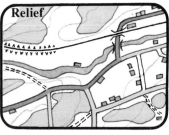

Relief

Relief or topographical maps are the most generally useful type of map, showing the physical details of the land.

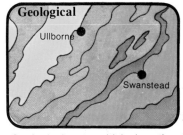

Geological

Geological maps, which show the arrangement of rocks in the earth's crust, are another example of the wide variety of maps available.

Making a map

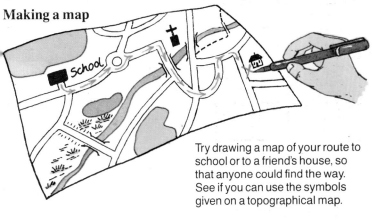

Try drawing a map of your route to school or to a friend's house, so that anyone could find the way. See if you can use the symbols given on a topographical map.

Map grids

Most topographical maps have a grid of squares on them. The lines are drawn at regular intervals and are numbered so you can refer to any point on the map and give its position. The numbered reference to the position of a feature is called the grid or map reference.

The lines going down the map are called "eastings" and those going across the map are called "northings." When you give a reference, give the easting number first, then the northing.

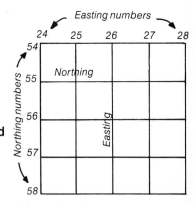

Always give the easting number that is on the *left* of the square and the northing number that is *below* the square you want to refer to.

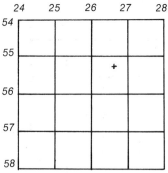

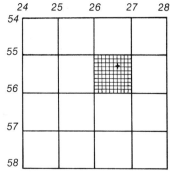

In the grid shown above, the grid reference of the square with the cross in is 2656. But when you use a map, you will usually want to refer to the exact position of a feature, not just the grid square it is in. You must imagine that each square is divided into tenths so that you can give a six-figure reference. To find the exact position of the cross, for example, you need to know how many tenths east of the easting it is. The answer is six, so the exact easting reference is 266. In the same way, you will see that the cross is seven tenths north of the northing, so the full northing reference is 567. The exact grid reference for the cross is therefore 266567.

How to make a grid measurer

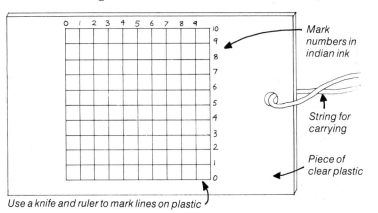

Mark numbers in indian ink

String for carrying

Piece of clear plastic

Use a knife and ruler to mark lines on plastic

Make yourself a grid measurer like this so you can read map references accurately by laying it over the appropriate grid square on your map. You need a small piece of clear plastic big enough to cover a grid square on your map. Mark a square on it the same size as the map grid squares and then divide it into equal tenths as shown.

Practise plotting

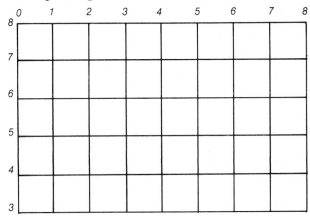

Practise plotting and have some fun! Plot out the map references on the right and then draw a line to join them up in the same order. You will see a picture appear.

3060, 1740, 1760, 8060, 6058, 6036, 5236, 5248, 3148, 3136, 2236, 2250, 0650, 1352, 0652, 0660, 1760. When you have finished, check your picture by turning to page 188.

Map scales

It would be impossible to draw a life-size map of an area, so to make maps a convenient size, everything is drawn scaled down to a fraction of its real size. The scale used is always given on a map so that you can work out actual distances and sizes of things. Large scale maps show a small area in great detail, and small scale maps show a larger area in less detail.

Actual size

Scale 1:2

Scale 1:10

If you draw something half its actual size, the scale of your picture will be 1:2. At a tenth of its size, the scale will be 1:10. Most walkers use 1:50,000 maps.

Your house

Your area street plan

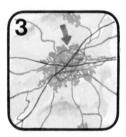

Your town

Your country

The Earth

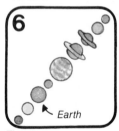

← *Earth*

The planets

To get an idea of what scale means, imagine that you live in the house arrowed in picture 1. Follow the sequence of pictures through and see how it gradually becomes harder, and then impossible, to pick out where you live as the scale of the pictures gets smaller.

Measuring distance

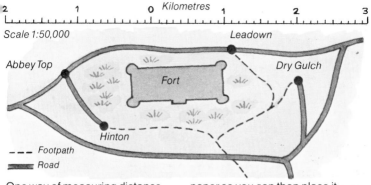

Scale 1:50,000

Abbey Top · Leadown · Dry Gulch · Fort · Hinton

- - - Footpath

■■■ Road

One way of measuring distance on a map is to use the straight edge of a piece of paper and lay it along the route, making a mark on the paper at any bends so that you can turn it without losing your place. Mark your starting and finishing points on the edge of the paper so you can then place it along the scale line on the map and read off the distance. Try using the plan and scale line above for practice, and work out the shortest route by road and on foot from Abbey Top to Dry Gulch. See page 188 for the answers.

More ways to measure distance

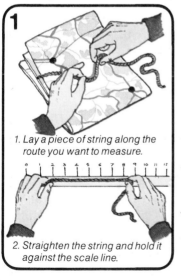

1. Lay a piece of string along the route you want to measure.

2. Straighten the string and hold it against the scale line.

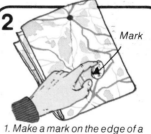

Mark

1. Make a mark on the edge of a coin with a felt pen.
2. Roll the coin along the route, counting the number of times the mark goes round.
3. Roll the coin along the scale line the same number of times to find the distance.

3 MAKE YOUR OWN MAP MEASURER (SEE NEXT PAGE)

27

How to make a map measurer

What you need

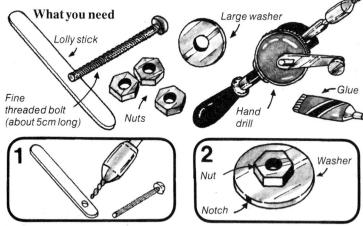

Lolly stick

Large washer

Fine threaded bolt (about 5cm long)

Nuts

Hand drill

Glue

1 Drill a hole through the lolly stick, close to one end and as big as the diameter of the bolt.

2 Nut

Washer

Notch

File a notch in the edge of the washer and then glue it to one of the nuts, making sure it is centred.

3 Thread the nut with the washer glued to it onto the far end of the bolt.

4 Lolly stick

Thread the other two nuts onto the bolt with the lolly stick between them, so that they hold it in place at the near end of the bolt.

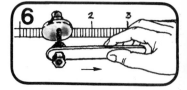

5 Before using the measurer, check that the washer is at the far end of the bolt. Then hold the stick so the notch is at the beginning of the distance you want to measure. Roll the washer along the route.

6 Place the measurer on the map scale and run it along the line so that the washer winds back up the bolt to its starting position. You can then read off the distance measured, next to the notch.

28

Map contours

Contour lines show you the shape of the land. They are lines on the map which join up points of land of the same height above sea level. They are drawn at regular height intervals, usually 20 metres. By looking at contours, you can see if the land is flat or hilly, with steep or shallow slopes.

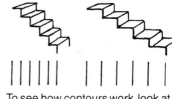

To see how contours work, look at these steps. Those on the left are steeper than those on the right as the steps are closer together. The contour lines drawn to represent them are also closer together.

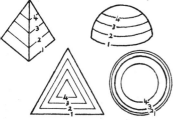

Different land forms are shown by the pattern of contours. If you were to look down on these shapes with lines drawn round them, you would see patterns of contours like those shown below the shapes.

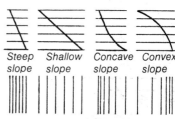

Steep slope   Shallow slope   Concave slope   Convex slope

The distance between contours tells you about the kinds of slope. Evenly spaced contours show that the land slopes evenly, but if the distance between contours varies, the slope varies.

Make a relief model of a hill

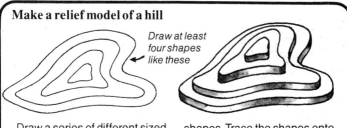

Draw at least four shapes like these

Draw a series of different sized, but similar shapes, either by tracing those above or by drawing your own, larger shapes. Trace the shapes onto thick cardboard, cut them out and glue them on top of one another.

Identifying land forms

In the pictures below, some common land forms are shown on the left and the contours that represent them are shown on the right.

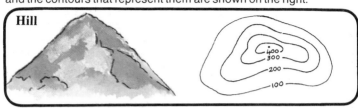

Hill

Volcano

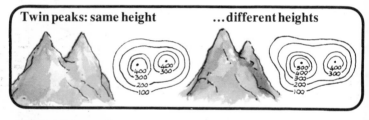

Twin peaks: same height   **...different heights**

Valley

Spur

Drawing a cross-section

Cross-sections will help you to find out more about the shape and slope of land. Try making a cross-section of the land between points A and B on the map below. Start by placing the straight edge of a piece of paper on the map so that it goes through A and B. Keep the paper steady and mark on where each contour crosses it, adding the height as shown.

On another piece of paper, draw a line the same length as A and B and then draw lines at 5 millimetre intervals above it, one for each contour height, as shown in picture 2. Mark the contour heights from your first piece of paper onto this with small crosses, then join up the crosses. The line you draw in will show a cross-section of the land forms in that area.

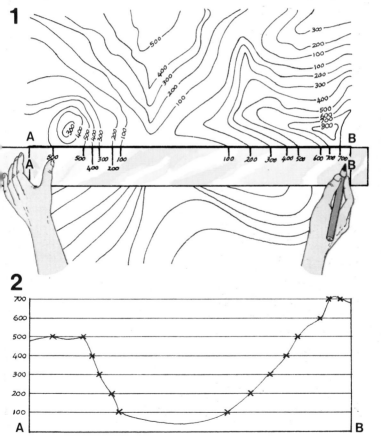

Compasses

Compasses tell you about direction. By using a compass, you can find the most direct route to an object, and you can get round an obstacle without losing your direction. All compasses are made up of two main parts: a small magnetized needle and a card or dial, like the one illustrated below, showing the compass points.

There are three main types of compass, although it may appear when you look around that there are many more, as they can have all sorts of attachments. Examples of the three main types are shown opposite. For normal map reading, a simple card compass is sufficient.

Compass points

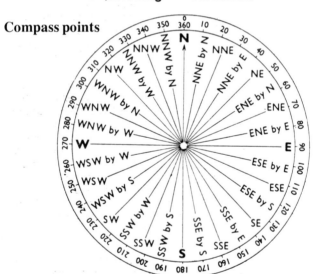

There are four main compass points: north, south, west and east. These are known as the cardinal points. North is the most important point in direction finding, and all the other points are based round it. So providing you know which direction is north, you will be able to find any direction you want. Altogether, there are 32 compass points. Naming them is known as "boxing the compass." The compass is also divided into 360 degrees. This is so that directions can be given very accurately to the nearest degree.

How a compass works

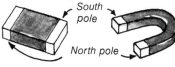
South pole

North pole

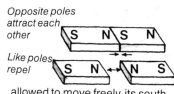
Opposite poles attract each other

Like poles repel

All magnets have a north and a south pole. Opposite poles are attracted to each other, so the north pole of one magnet will attract the south pole of another. The earth is a huge magnet (see page 36), so if a small magnet is allowed to move freely, its south pole will be attracted to the earth's north pole. This is why the magnetized compass needle always settles in a north-south line and is an accurate direction indicator.

1

This compass has a needle spinning freely on the end of a pin, which stands in the centre of a fixed card showing the compass points. The whole compass has to be turned round to get a compass reading.

2

Card compass

In this type, the needle is fixed to the underside of the card, which spins freely. The card's movement is controlled by the magnetic movement of the needle. As the needle lies along the north-south line on the card, the card always turns to north, so compass readings can be made without turning the compass. Pages 34-5 show you how to make a compass of this type.

3

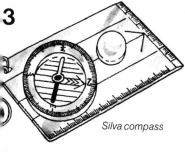
Silva compass

The third type of compass has the needle on the card and floating in a liquid. This is more useful than the other compasses, as the liquid makes the needle settle down more quickly and stops it moving as much, so you can get a faster and more accurate reading. The Silva compass shown here is one example of this type of compass.

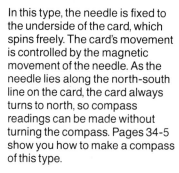

How to make a card compass

What you need

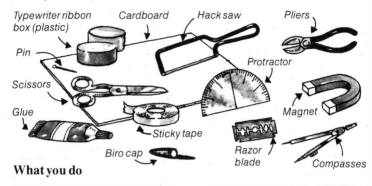

Typewriter ribbon box (plastic)
Cardboard
Hack saw
Pliers
Pin
Protractor
Scissors
Glue
Sticky tape
Magnet
Biro cap
Razor blade
Compasses

What you do

Place the protractor on the piece of cardboard and make a mark at the edge of it every 5°. Turn the protractor over and continue marking every 5° to make a circle.

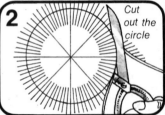

Cut out the circle

Draw a straight line inwards from each 5° mark. Then use the compasses to draw a circle with a diameter 8 mm less than that of the plastic box.

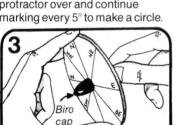

Biro cap

Mark the cardinal points onto the card circle. Use the saw to cut the top off the biro cap so it is about a centimetre shorter than the box depth. Cut a hole in the circle just big enough to fit the biro cap.

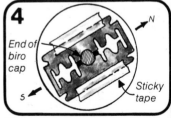

End of biro cap

N

S

Sticky tape

Fasten the razor blade to the underside of the card circle with sticky tape, positioning it so that it lies along the north-south line marked on the top side of the card.

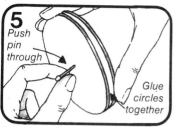

5 Push pin through

Glue circles together

On the remaining cardboard, draw two more circles small enough to just fit in the box. Cut them out and glue them together. Push the pin through the centre of the circles.

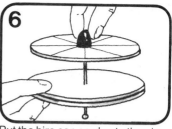

6

Put the biro cap card onto the pin. Adjust the length of the pin by pushing it further through the two circles or pulling it back until the top spins clear of the base.

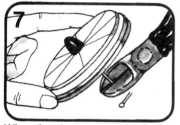

7

When the pin is the right length, use the pliers to cut off the spare end of it sticking through the bottom of the base. Make sure that the rough end left behind does not stick out below the cardboard.

8

Stroke the razor blade with one end of the magnet, in one direction only. Then balance the card on the pin and see if north points in the direction of north. If it points south instead, you need to stroke the magnet along the razor blade again, using the same end of it but stroking in the opposite direction.

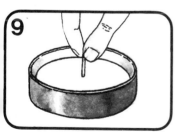

9

Glue the circles with the pin into the base of the box and then balance the top card with the biro cap onto the pin again. The card compass is now ready for use.

Using a compass

To be able to use a compass you need to know how to take "bearings." A bearing is the direction of an object in relation to north, from where you are standing. It is always given in degrees and is measured clockwise from north. As the pictures below show, there are actually three north points. Bearings can be based on any of these, but magnetic bearings are used most often.

Bearing is 45°N

To take a bearing with a card compass, hold the compass flat and look towards the object, in this case a wind pump. Imagine a straight line from it to the centre of your compass. Count the number of degrees from the north point to this line to get the magnetic bearing.

North points

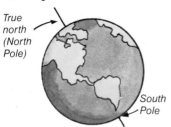
True north (North Pole)
South Pole

True north is the direction of the North Pole, that is, the north end of the axis on which the earth spins. Weathervanes on church steeples point to true north.

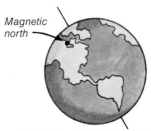
Magnetic north

Magnetic north is the magnetic north pole of the earth, situated in the Hudson Bay area of Canada. It moves a little each year, and the amount it moves is shown on maps.

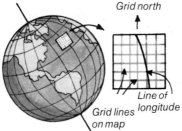
Grid north
Line of longitude
Grid lines on map

Grid north is the north on maps indicated by the vertical grid lines. As the grid is flat and the earth's surface is curved, the grid lines do not run true north. To see this, look where the lines of longitude are marked at the top and bottom of a map and see how they would curve across the grid if drawn in.

Magnetic north → ↑ Grid north → True north

A map key shows the three norths like this and tells you the angle between magnetic and true north, called the "magnetic variation." Because the magnetic north pole moves very slightly each year, the magnetic variation changes a little annually. The variation and the amount by which it changes is shown on the map under the north points.

With a compass you will take magnetic bearings, but on a map you may use true or magnetic bearings. You can convert one to the other by using the magnetic variation. To change true to magnetic bearings you add the variation to your bearing, and to change magnetic to true bearings you subtract the variation.

How to avoid an obstacle

1

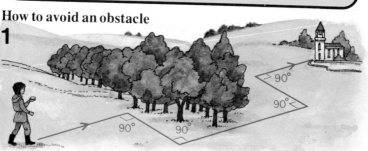

Use your compass to get round an obstruction, such as a thick wood, without losing your route. Walk at 90° to your route, counting how many paces you take to pass the obstacle. Turn back 90° onto your original bearing and walk past the obstacle, then turn 90° again and walk the same number of paces to get back onto your original route.

2

Another way to avoid an obstacle is to walk at 60° to your route, counting your paces. Turn back at 60° when you are past the obstacle, and count the same number of paces to return to your route.

Map and compass

To find your way quickly and accurately you need both a map and a compass. The map is for planning a route, and the compass is for following bearings which you take on the map or ground. A compass is also used to "orientate" a map and to find your position on the map if you are not sure where you are.

Orientating the map

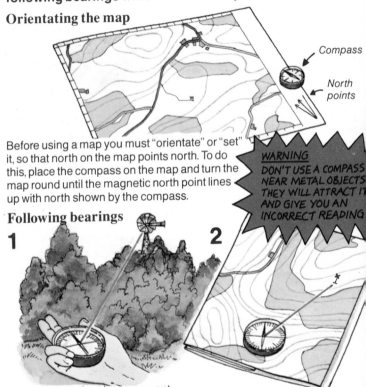

Compass

North points

Before using a map you must "orientate" or "set" it, so that north on the map points north. To do this, place the compass on the map and turn the map round until the magnetic north point lines up with north shown by the compass.

WARNING
DON'T USE A COMPASS NEAR METAL OBJECTS THEY WILL ATTRACT IT AND GIVE YOU AN INCORRECT READING

Following bearings

1

2

If you can see the place you want to get to, take a compass bearing to it and then follow this bearing. Even though you can see your objective when you start, you must take a bearing in case trees or hills obscure your view later.

If you can't see the place you want to get to but know your position on the map, place the compass on your position on the map and take a bearing to your objective. Follow this bearing.

Finding your position

1

If you are not sure of your exact position on the map you can find it by using your compass. First select two or, if possible, three features on the ground in front of you, which you can identify on the map. Then take a compass bearing to each of these features.

2

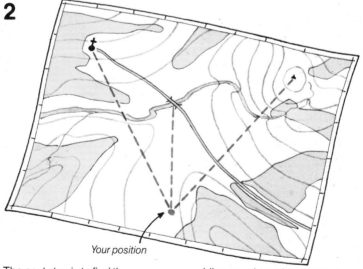

Your position

The next step is to find the backbearings of these features, that is, the bearings from the features back to your position, by adding or subtracting 180° to the bearings (see page 47). Draw the backbearings onto the map. Your position is where they cross.

Map orientating without compas

As long as you have a map and compass with you, you should never get lost because you can orientate the map and find your position on it by using the compass. If you don't have a compass, you can still orientate your map by matching features on it with those in front of you on the ground. If there are no distinct features because, for example, you are in a forest, you can orientate your map by finding north and lining it up with the true north point on the map. You can use the sun to find north with a watch or shadow stick.

Orientating your map in a town or city is easy. Simply align the map with the streets in front of you.

In the country you can orientate a map by choosing two or more features on the ground and then turning the map until they line up with their positions on the map.

Using the sun

If you are in the northern hemisphere, point the hour hand at the sun. South is midway between the hour hand and twelve.

In the southern hemisphere, north is midway between the hour hand and twelve, when twelve o'clock points to the sun.

In places using British Summer Time, south is midway between one and the hour hand, if the hour hand points to the sun.

Using a shadow stick

1 Clear a flat area of ground and place a stick upright in the middle of it. Mark the path of the stick's shadow over the next hour by placing a small object, such as a stone, at the end of the shadow about every ten minutes.

2 With another stick and a length of string, scratch a circle on the ground like this, starting from the longest shadow you have marked. If the ground is too hard to scratch, try using string or more stones to mark out the circle.

3 Continue marking where the shadow curve would go so that it cuts the circle again. Don't wait for the sun to make more shadows, estimate the rest of the curve.

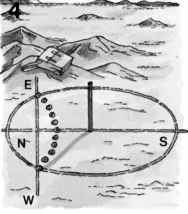

4 A line drawn between the two places where the curve cuts the circle will point east-west. North-south is at right angles to this through the base of the stick.

Finding direction by the stars

On a clear night, the stars are a useful guide to finding north. In the northern hemisphere, a star called the Pole Star shows the direction of true north as it is almost directly over the North Pole. It is not quite so easy in the southern hemisphere. There is no star over the South Pole, and you must use a group of stars called the Southern Cross to find south.

Southern hemisphere

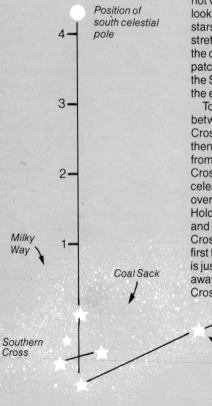

Position of south celestial pole

4 —

3 —

2 —

Milky Way

1 —

Coal Sack

Southern Cross

Although the Southern Cross is made up of four bright stars, it is not very easy to spot. To find it, look along the misty band of small stars, called the Milky Way, that stretches across the sky, and find the dark patch with no stars. This patch is called the Coal Sack, and the Southern Cross lies right on the edge of it.

To find true south, imagine a line between the two stars of the Cross that are farthest apart and then follow this line across the sky from the star at the foot of the Cross. It points towards the south celestial pole, that is, to a position over the south pole of the earth. Hold out your hand at arm's length and measure the length of the Cross between your thumb and first finger. The south celestial pole is just over four times this length away from the foot of the Southern Cross.

Look for these two stars called "pointers" to make sure you have found the Southern Cross. They lie in a straight line with the top star of the Cross on the left side of it.

Northern hemisphere

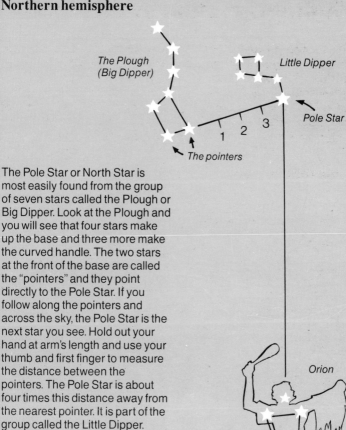

The Plough (Big Dipper)

Little Dipper

Pole Star

The pointers

Orion

Orion's belt

The Pole Star or North Star is most easily found from the group of seven stars called the Plough or Big Dipper. Look at the Plough and you will see that four stars make up the base and three more make the curved handle. The two stars at the front of the base are called the "pointers" and they point directly to the Pole Star. If you follow along the pointers and across the sky, the Pole Star is the next star you see. Hold out your hand at arm's length and use your thumb and first finger to measure the distance between the pointers. The Pole Star is about four times this distance away from the nearest pointer. It is part of the group called the Little Dipper.

Another way of finding north is from Orion, a group of stars which can be easily spotted by the three bright stars that form Orion's belt. If you imagine Orion as a figure, the small star that represents his head will point to the Pole Star.

Planning a route

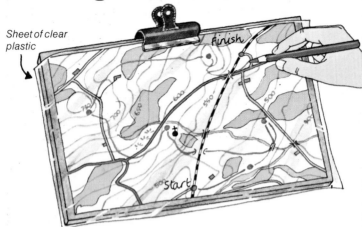

Sheet of clear plastic

Finish

700 800 600 550 500 400

Start

It is important to plan a route thoroughly before you set out hiking. Start by fixing a sheet of clear plastic over a map of the area you are going to. Use a chinagraph pencil to mark on the places you want to visit and your starting and finishing points. You can then work out the best route between these points. Do study the map carefully and remember to consider the following things:

Points to remember

1

The most direct route may not be the easiest. Look for obstructions such as marsh, which you will need to avoid, and do check any symbols used on the map if you are not sure of their meaning.

2 Measure the distance you are planning to walk (see page 27). You should know roughly how fast you walk, so that you can work out how long the route will take you.

3 Remember to allow time for things such as sightseeing and eating. You must be realistic about how far you can go in a day, especially if it is your first visit to an area.

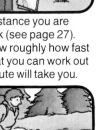

4 Walking over rough ground or in woods takes longer than walking along paths or over short grass in fields. Allow for this when you work out how far you can go.

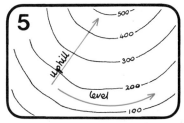

5 It is usually easier to walk on level ground than uphill. If your route follows a single contour it will be on level ground. The more nearly at right angles to contours it is, the steeper it will be.

Time	Place	Map reference	Bearings	Distance
9.40 am	Tolton Station	486125		
10.15 am	Wharf Castle	451167	282°N	2.3 Km
12.40 pm	Oldbury Caves	462210	23°N	3.8 km
2.45 pm	Evesham Village	497174	125°N	1.7 Km
4.10 pm	Tolton Station	486125	210°N	2.5 km

Once you have decided on the best route, make a route card like this showing the places you intend to visit and your route between them. Include bearings and map grid references, and the time you expect to reach each place. Leave a copy with someone at home.

Walking a route

Keep your map orientated and compare it to the landscape as you go along so you always know where you are on it. But don't allow yourself to be dominated by your map and compass or you will not see anything around you. Before you set out, make sure your map-reading equipment is well organized so you will not lose time searching through pockets for things you need.

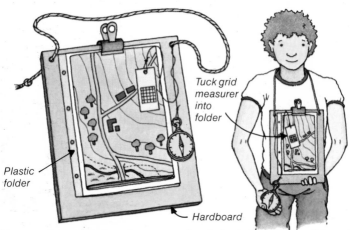

Plastic folder

Hardboard

Tuck grid measurer into folder

Always put your map in a clear plastic folder or bag to keep it dry. It is a good idea to attach it to a piece of hardboard or plywood with a bulldog clip. You can make two holes in the board and thread a piece of string through so you can hang it round your neck. Tie your compass and grid measurer to the board as well.

A pedometer measures the distance you walk. It is useful for working out how fast you walk over different types of ground so you can plan a route accurately. Before using it, set the dial to your normal stride length. The pedometer counts the number of strides you take and converts this figure into the distance you have walked.

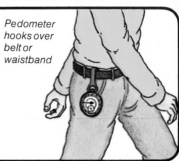

Pedometer hooks over belt or waistband

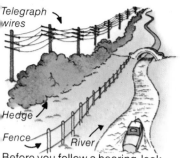

Telegraph wires

Hedge

Fence

River

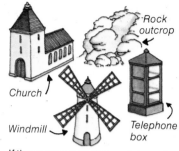

Rock outcrop

Church

Windmill

Telephone box

Before you follow a bearing, look at the map to see if there are any features along it like those shown above. If there are, you can find your way easily by following them.

If there are no such "continuous" features, you can find your way by looking for landmarks like these on your route and then taking a bearing from each one to the next.

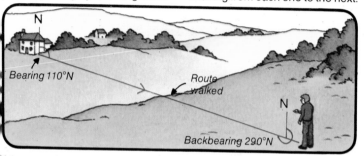

Bearing 110°N

Route walked

Backbearing 290°N

If there are few landmarks ahead, you can check that you are not wandering off your bearing by taking a backbearing. This is the bearing back to the last landmark on your route. The backbearing should be the same as your bearing plus 180° if the bearing is less than 180,° or minus 180° if it is more. For example, if the person in

the picture decided to walk on a bearing of 110°N from the house, his backbearing would be 290°N (110°N + 180°N). If it was either more or less than this, he would know that to get on the right bearing, he needed to walk either to the left or to the right by the number of degrees difference between his backbearing and 290.°

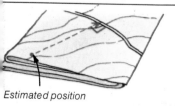

Estimated position

If you are not sure of your position on the map, orientate it and then look for roads on it. If there is a road or crossroads near where you think you are, take a bearing on the map at right angles to it and head in that direction.

Difficult and dangerous terrains

In the desert

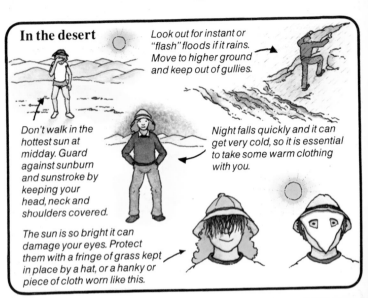

Look out for instant or "flash" floods if it rains. Move to higher ground and keep out of gullies.

Don't walk in the hottest sun at midday. Guard against sunburn and sunstroke by keeping your head, neck and shoulders covered.

Night falls quickly and it can get very cold, so it is essential to take some warm clothing with you.

The sun is so bright it can damage your eyes. Protect them with a fringe of grass kept in place by a hat, or a hanky or piece of cloth worn like this.

In forests

Keep alert, and beware of animals that may be dangerous.

Keep your arms and legs covered for protection against insects and undergrowth.

You can't see far in woods or forests, so it is difficult to see map reference points. Mark your path with signs like these as you go along so you can find your way back if you get lost.

On moorland and high ground

It is difficult to judge distances as there are few distinct features to refer to.

The higher you go, the colder and more windy it becomes. Take warm, windproof clothing.

Bogs and marshes are dangerous. Learn to recognize marsh plants so you know which areas to avoid.

Bright clothing will help you to be seen and to see each other.

REMEMBER
IF YOU MUST CROSS MARSH, TEST GROUND WITH A STICK FIRST AND MARK YOUR ROUTE

On the seashore

HELP!

Make sure it is safe before you go in the water. There might be dangerous animals or strong currents.

Find out the times of high tides before you walk on beaches so you don't get trapped by incoming tides.

Sharks

Portuguese Man-o'-War

Sea Urchins

In the mountains

Don't go without an experienced person and the right gear.

If you think you are lost

If you get lost, first check that you have tried all the tips for walking a route suggested on page 47. Look around for landmarks or features to help you find your position on the map (see page 39). Then, if you still don't know where you are, either try to retrace your steps, or try the ideas shown here for finding help.

Look...

...at your map and orientate it with your compass.

...for prominent landmarks, then try to find them on the map.

Smell...

...the sea

...smoke from a bonfire or industry

Listen...

...for traffic noise: car engines, horns and radios.

...for the sound of water such as rivers or waves.

TAKE CARE IF YOU FOLLOW A RIVER IN HILL COUNTRY. YOU CAN SUDDENLY FIND YOURSELF FACED WITH A VERTICAL CLIFF WHERE THE ROCKS MAY BE WET AND SLIPPERY FROM SPRAY

...for a hill or a tree to climb. You will see further from a high point and may spot something to guide you.

...at night for the glow of light from a town or for car headlights, which show from a great distance away.

...farm animals and silage

...exhaust fumes from traffic

...for machines.

...for church bells or clocks chiming.

...for animal noises like dogs barking.

51

Understanding the weather

Weather is very important in all outdoor activities. Before you go on a day's hike or bicycle ride, you should always check the weather forecast for the day.

These pages will help you understand how weather is caused by a combination of the sun's heat, water, and the earth's atmosphere. They will also show you how to forecast the weather using weather maps.

Clouds, rain and snow

The sun heats the earth, and the earth then warms the air above it. Warm air rises because it is light; as it rises, it cools. In the end, it becomes so cold and heavy that it sinks down again.

Warm air can hold more moisture than cold air. When warm, moist air cools, some of its moisture condenses out and makes droplets of water. Fog, mist and clouds are made of these droplets.

The drops of condensation on bathroom windows come from moisture that condensed out of warm moist air when it touched the cold windowpanes and cooled.

Moisture condenses on cold window

Snowflake

Cloud forms as warm, moist air rises and cools

Warm air rises from towns and cities

Some clouds, like cumulonimbus, are made of ice particles as well as water droplets. The ice particles grow bigger because the water droplets freeze onto them. They turn into ice crystals, which join up and make snowflakes. The snowflakes are heavy enough to fall out of the cloud. If they melt on the way down, they fall as rain.

Other, lower clouds, like stratus, are made only of water droplets. The droplets bump into each other and join up, making larger water drops. The biggest, heaviest drops fall out of the cloud as raindrops.

Depressions and anticyclones

Pressure is measured with an instrument like this called a barometer

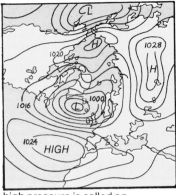

Air sinking onto the earth's surface creates high pressure. Air rising above the surface creates low pressure.

Pressure is shown on weather maps by lines called isobars. Isobars join places with the same pressure. An area of low pressure is called a depression; an area of high pressure is called an anticyclone. Depressions and anticyclones are marked by closed, more or less circular isobars. Depressions tend to bring unsettled, rainy or snowy weather. Anticyclones usually bring warm, settled weather in summer, and fog or very cold, clear weather in winter.

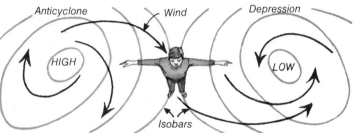

Areas of high and low pressure tend to even up in the same way that water flows through open lock gates until it is the same level on both sides. Wind is air moving from high to low pressure areas. The greater the difference in pressure, the closer the isobars will be, and the faster the winds will blow. Air moves in a spiral, blowing clockwise away from anticyclones and anticlockwise towards depressions, in the northern hemisphere. The opposite is true in the southern hemisphere.

If you stand with your back to the wind, the lower pressure will be on your left in the northern hemisphere, but on your right in the southern hemisphere. If you can see stormy weather in the high pressure direction, for example, you can expect it to come your way soon.

53

What weather maps show you

Weather maps tell you about weather conditions over a wide or a small area. Many use symbols to show wind speed and direction, and temperature, or sunshine, fog, rain and snow. Some are marked by isobars, and show depressions, fronts and anticyclones. Try looking at weather maps in newspapers and on television to see if you can understand them.

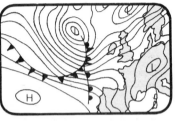

This is the kind of weather map which is often printed in newspapers. It shows a depression and some fronts. A depression tends to form where a mass of warm, moist air meets a mass of colder, drier air. Clouds form along the boundary lines between the two types of air. These lines are called fronts.

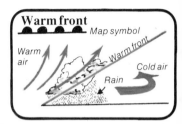

A warm front is the line where warm air meets cold air and rises over it. The first signs of a warm front are cirrus clouds, then cirrostratus, altostratus and nimbostratus. There is also a drop in pressure. Warm fronts take a long time to pass. They bring rain or snow.

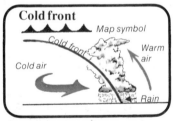

A cold front is the line where cold air meets warm air and pushes underneath it, lifting it up. Cold fronts pass quickly; they bring cumulus, cumulonimbus, cirrostratus and altostratus clouds, with heavy showers of rain, snow or hail. They can also bring thunder and lightning.

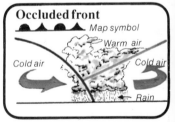

An occluded front is the line where cold and warm fronts meet and join up. It brings a combination of warm and cold front weather conditions: long periods of rain, drizzle or snow, and thick, low clouds.

Wind speed

Anticyclones are associated with calm weather, whereas depressions bring changeable, windy weather. The pictures on this page show a scale of wind speed called the Beaufort Scale, after its inventor.

Under each picture is the description of the wind and its effect, and its map symbol. The Beaufort number or force of the wind is shown in the top left corner of each picture.

Calm ⊙
No wind; smoke rises vertically

Light air
Wind direction shown by smoke, not by wind vanes

Light breeze
Leaves rustle; wind vanes are moved by wind

Gentle breeze
Wind extends a light flag; leaves move all the time

Moderate breeze
Wind raises dust and paper; small branches move

Fresh breeze
Small crested waves form on inland water; small trees sway

Strong breeze
Umbrellas are difficult to use; large branches begin to move

Moderate gale
Whole trees in motion; some difficulty in walking against the wind

Fresh gale
Twigs break off trees; great difficulty in walking against the wind

Strong gale
Slight damage to buildings: chimney pots and slates removed

Whole gale
Rare inland. Trees uprooted; extensive damage to buildings

Storm
Very rare. Widespread damage to buildings etc.

Clouds

Cirrus—streaks of high cloud, made of ice crystals. It looks like wisps or strands of hair.

Cirrostratus—a thin veil of high cloud which can create "haloes" (rings) around the sun or moon.

Cirrocumulus—a mackerel sky. Fine, rippling lines of high clouds, made of ice crystals.

Altostratus—like cirrostratus, but thicker and lower; it blurs the sun. A plain, grey cloud layer.

Nimbostratus—a dark, grey rain cloud. A thick, low form of altostratus.

Altocumulus—rows of fluffy, round clouds; lumpier and lower in the sky than cirrocumulus.

Altocumulus castellanus—clouds in long rows, like battlements. Can mean a thunderstorm ahead.

Stratus—a very low, thick cloud layer; fog is stratus cloud resting on the ground.

Fair weather cumulus—tiny puffs of white cloud, formed by "bubbles" of warm, rising air.

Cumulonimbus—the thundercloud. Flat base and towering top. It brings showers of rain, hail or snow.

Stratocumulus—long rolls of clouds; they can form a low, white patchwork. A sign of clearer, drier weather.

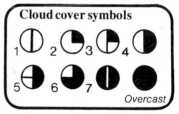

Cloud cover symbols

Overcast

Weather men use these symbols to show how much of the sky is covered by cloud. The sky is divided into eighths, called oktas. So if half of the sky is covered by cloud, cloud amount is four oktas.

Signs of good and bad weather

Some people don't bother with weather forecasts, they use natural signs to predict the weather. You can get an idea of what kind of weather to expect for the day if you look for these signs, but do listen to the forecast and study weather maps as well.

Fine weather

Signs of fine weather are: smoke rising up in morning haze; dewy grass under a clear morning sky; birds flying high.

Rain and stormy weather

Signs of wet weather are: stars twinkling more than usual; animals behaving restlessly in fields; insects flying near the ground; swallows and other insect-eating birds diving low.

Recording what you see

Whenever you go exploring, keep a record of the things you see and do. You will find it interesting and useful to look back over and to show to family and friends.

In writing

Make daily notes during your journey. Include information such as possible future camp sites and places you would like to visit. When you get home, buy a loose-leaf file and write up all your notes in it. Keep your route card in the file and your map. Make an index to keep at the front.

Map in plastic folder

In pictures

Try sketching things you see on route, then colour the sketches later with crayons or watercolour paints. If you have a camera, take photographs of things that interest you. Prints can be mounted in your file on pages opposite the appropriate notes. Slides can be used for your own "film show."

In sounds

If you have a cassette recorder or can borrow one, try recording a commentary of your journey instead of making notes. You can also record noises along the route such as bird song, sea or river sounds, crowd noises, trains or machinery. When you get home, use the recording together with your prints or slides.

MOO

59

Food

Always take some food on day hikes as you will get hungry walking. The pictures below show the types of food you can carry easily. Delicious, high energy fruit bars are also good for walkers.

In warm weather take cold food such as sandwiches or salads, and fresh fruit. Don't forget to take a soft fruit drink or water as well.

To travel light, take a selection of high energy foods such as nuts, dried fruit, chocolate, and oatmeal blocks or wholemeal biscuits.

If you want hot food, there is a good choice of dehydrated meals. They need about 20 minutes soaking and 10 to 15 minutes cooking. Don't forget to take water with you.

Freeze-dried food is light to carry and very easy to prepare. It simply needs mixing with hot or cold water, which can be added straight to the foil packet. It is ready to eat after about five minutes.

Cooking

Most convenient for cooking on day hikes is a gas cartridge stove (shown here), a methylated spirit stove or a solid fuel stove.

If you use a fire for cooking, make quite sure you put it out after use by sprinkling water on it like this until it is cold to touch.

How to make fruit bars

What you need

50 grams of milk powder

1 tablespoon of lemon juice

Mincer

100 grams of mixed nuts

300 grams of mixed dried fruit

50 grams of ground almonds

2 sheets of rice paper

1 Add more juice if needed

Mince or chop fruit and nuts finely and mix to a paste with lemon juice, ground almonds and milk powder.

2 Rice paper

Put mixture on a sheet of rice paper and roll out until it is about eight millimetres thick.

3

Cover with another sheet of rice paper and put in the refrigerator for several hours.

4

Cut fruit mixture into bars and store wrapped in grease-proof paper or aluminium foil.

Variations on basic recipe

① 50g milk powder
50g ground almonds
1 tbsp lemon juice
100g prunes
100g currants
100g raisins
50g ginger (fresh or preserved)
1 tbsp honey

② 50g milk powder
50g ground almonds
1 tbsp orange juice
orange rind
100g dates
100g raisins
50g prunes
50g walnuts
50g chocolate

Orienteering

Orienteering is a popular sport in many countries. It is a test of map reading and compass skills. The idea is to find your way across country, visiting a series of control points in a fixed order. The control points are marked by red and white buckets or nylon markers. At each one there is a punch for marking the special card that you carry to show you have found the controls. The person completing the course in the fastest time is the winner.

Ruin	Building	Uncrossable fence	Crossable fence	Wall
		Gate		
Path	Cart track	Road	Marsh	Stream
Small Large			Open Wooded	Small Large
Boulder field	Boulder	Impassable cliff	Pit	Contours
Easy to cross Slow	Small Large		V	

Orienteering maps are special, very large scale topographical maps. They are designed to give as much detail as possible. Special symbols are used, a few of which are shown here.

Types of event

1 Cross-country orienteering

Cross-country orienteering is the main type of event. Competitors set off at intervals to copy the position of control points from a master map onto their own map. They have to navigate from each control point to the next. The winner is the person who reaches the finish in the fastest time, having visited all the control points in the right order.

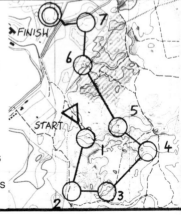

Equipment

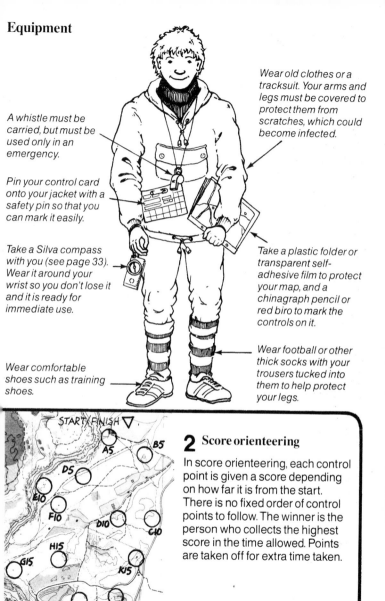

A whistle must be carried, but must be used only in an emergency.

Pin your control card onto your jacket with a safety pin so that you can mark it easily.

Take a Silva compass with you (see page 33). Wear it around your wrist so you don't lose it and it is ready for immediate use.

Wear comfortable shoes such as training shoes.

Wear old clothes or a tracksuit. Your arms and legs must be covered to protect them from scratches, which could become infected.

Take a plastic folder or transparent self-adhesive film to protect your map, and a chinagraph pencil or red biro to mark the controls on it.

Wear football or other thick socks with your trousers tucked into them to help protect your legs.

2 Score orienteering

In score orienteering, each control point is given a score depending on how far it is from the start. There is no fixed order of control points to follow. The winner is the person who collects the highest score in the time allowed. Points are taken off for extra time taken.

Age groups

Almost anyone can take part in orienteering events. Competitions are held between people of the same age group. Courses are planned to take a certain time to run rather than be of a fixed length.

Approx. length	Time	Class Men	Age range	Class Women	Time	Approx. length
1-2 km	25 mins	M10	10 and under	W10	25 mins	1-2 km
2-3 km	30 mins	M12	11-12	W12	30 mins	2-3 km
2.5-4 km	40 mins	M13	13-14	W13	35 mins	2-3.5 km
3-5 km	50 mins	M15	15-16	W15	40 mins	2.5-4 km
4-7 km	60 mins	M17	17-18	W17	60 mins	3-5.5 km
6-10 km	70 mins	M19	19-20			
			19-34	W19	75 mins	5-8 km
6-14 km	90 mins	M21	21-34			
6-8 km	75 mins	M35	35-42	W35	60 mins	2.5-4 km
4-7 km	70 mins	M43	43-49	W43	50 mins	2-3.5 km
3-5 km	60 mins	M50	50-56	W50	50 mins	2-3 km
3-5 km	60 mins	M56	57 and over	W56	50 mins	2-3 km

The chart above shows the age classes and maximum course lengths.

1 What to do at an event

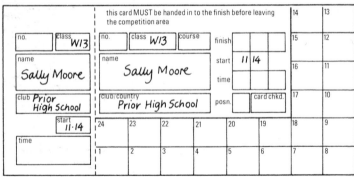

On the day of the event for which you have entered, report in as soon as you arrive. You will be given a control card like this, a map of the course area, a control descriptions sheet and your starting time. The control descriptions sheet tells you what the controls are, such as a path junction or a gate, and gives the code numbers of the controls. Fill in your name and other details on the control card.

A few minutes before your starting time your equipment will be checked and you will have to hand in your control card stub, so that the officials have a record of those taking part in the event.

At the starting signal, run to the master map and copy down the controls for your age group course onto your own map. It helps if you link them with straight lines. Think carefully about your route, but move off quickly.

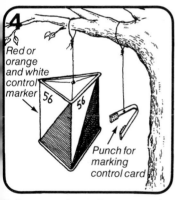

Red or orange and white control marker

56 56

Punch for marking control card

Follow your planned route round the course regardless of where other people go. The controls look like this. Always check the code number with your control descriptions to see that you have found the correct control. Don't forget to punch your control card.

Always report to the finish and hand over your control card, even if you don't complete the course. Otherwise a search party will be sent out and may spend hours looking for you while you are safely at home.

Hints for beginners

	Paths	Light vegetation	Heavy vegetation
Level ground			
Uphill			
Downhill			

Learn to estimate the distance you have travelled, so you will know your position on the map even when you are in country with few features. Make a chart like this of the number of paces you take to cover 100 metres walking or running on level ground and going uphill and downhill. Do this for different types of terrain.

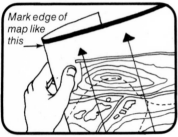

Mark edge of map like this →

The grid lines on orienteering maps point to magnetic north, so you don't have to waste time converting map bearings. Mark the north edge of the map so it is still easy to see if you fold the map.

You can also use your Silva compass to keep the map orientated. Remember that the most important thing is to know where you are on the ground and map all the time.

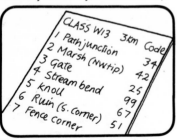

CLASS W13 3km
1 Path junction   Code
2 Marsh (NW tip)   34
3 Gate   42
4 Stream bend   25
5 Knoll   99
6 Ruin (S. corner)   67
7 Fence corner   51

This is what a control descriptions sheet looks like. You might find it saves time to write the control descriptions onto your control card in the correct boxes.

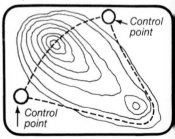

Control point

Control point

Try to spot possible routes between controls. Think whether it will be better to go over a hill, or round it on flatter ground. Look out for marsh and other obstacles.

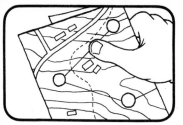

Get used to reading the map without having north at the top, so you can keep it turned to fit the ground ahead. Try using your thumb to mark your position.

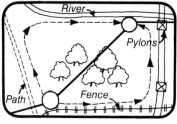

It is essential to know where you are on the map all the time. Try to follow "handrail features", such as rivers, ridges, fences, pylons and paths, wherever possible.

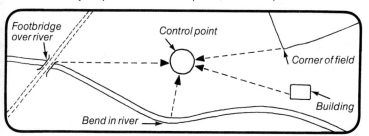

When you get near to a control, try to find an "attack point". This is a feature, such as a road junction or the corner of a field, which can be located easily on the ground and helps to take you close to the control point without much chance of error. Don't panic if you can't find the control point. Go back to the attack point and try again.

Never follow other competitors as they may be looking for a different control, and may even be on another course. Never ask for information, and approach another competitor only if you are totally lost.

After an event, talk to other competitors about the routes they chose between control points. Study your map and see how many routes you can spot between controls. Did you always make the right choice?

About camping

The following section of this book (up to page 130) is about camping and the fun that can be had from living outdoors. Many people think that a lot of expensive equipment is needed for camping, but this is not true. It is quite easy to camp safely using ordinary household items and only a little special equipment.

These pages are intended as a guide to help you get started. Once you have gained experience, you will discover you own ways of doing things.

Later on, you may want to become adventurous and camp in extreme conditions such as mountains, deserts or heathlands. But remember, this should not be attempted without expert guidance and until you have had a lot of experience of camping.

How to start

If your house has a garden, you can start by camping out overnight with a friend. You will be amazed at the noises you notice and the change in the temperature.

If you go on holiday with your parents, you could camp while they stay in a hotel or caravan. It would be cheaper for them and more fun for you.

When you have some experience of camping, look for sites on private land not too far from home where you can camp for a weekend.

As you gain more experience, you can safely camp further away from home and stay for longer periods. Always make sure to tell your parents where you are going.

Before you go camping you should do some cooking. Practise at home in the kitchen to find out which dishes are easiest to make.

If possible, cook in the garden with a camp stove and make a list of things you use. You can't pop back into the kitchen when camping.

Finding and choosing a site

Before you pick a site, think about the kind of place you want to camp in and what you want to do there. You might want to be near the sea or near good walking country, or you might want to go bird-watching. Let your interests guide you.

First look at a map of the area you have chosen, to try and spot possible sites. If you can, visit the area before you go camping.

It is a good idea to travel through the area by train, as you may see sites that are not easily accessible from a road.

You can see more from a bus than a car because it's higher up. So if you can't get a train, look around the area on a local bus.

If you are cycling, stop and ask local people about possible sites. As a last resort, you could look at a book of camp sites.

When you have found a site, first see if you can get permission to camp there from the owner. If he agrees, you can then go and select the best position to camp.

Start by trying to imagine the site under the worst possible weather conditions. If you are able to, visit it in the depths of winter.

Select a level site, not one at the bottom of a slope. It might rain.

If you camp on a slope, you will wake up at one end of your tent, or outside it.

Choose a place away from cliffs or trees to avoid falling objects.

Look for a sheltered site, near bushes or a bank.

Consider the distance between the site and the nearest water supply.

Try to avoid a site downwind from farm animal buildings, because of the smell.

Look for signs that tell you which way the wind usually blows, e.g. trees bent over.

A good position to pitch your tent is on a raised area. It is quite likely to be the driest site and it will be the one with the best view.

Look for signs of marshy ground, such as plants that normally live in wet areas. A site near stagnant water will attract biting insects.

Never camp in a dry gully. Whole expeditions have been swept away by sudden floods.

Types of camp: standing...

Before you go camping, you need to decide how long you are going for and what kind of camp you want it to be. There are two main types of camp, called standing and lightweight camps.

A standing camp is one in which you pitch your tent on one site for the whole camp. The position of the site is particularly important as the camp will be a base from which to go out for day trips.

When you first go camping, it is best to start with short standing camps to get experience. If you go for a weekend you can easily take with you all the food and clothing you will need. A longer camp needs more planning. You will have to consider washing clothes, and if you are not camping near shops, you will need a larger store of food. You will also need to make proper toilet facilities and to think about what you will do with rubbish.

When you choose a standing camp site, try to consider everyone's interests. Aim to mix visits to towns and museums with trips to the river or sea.

. . . and lightweight

Lightweight camping is for those who like to travel around, staying only one or two nights at each site. As the name suggests, the idea is to keep weight to a minimum, as it is no fun hiking with a heavy rucksack. You take only the most essential equipment, and it must be as light and compact as possible.

This kind of camping is not really suitable for beginners. You must be skilled at pitching your tent quickly in any weather and you must be able to use a map and compass for finding your way.

If you do go lightweight camping, it is best to go with a friend. You will be able to share equipment, such as the tent and cooking pots, so that you have less to carry. But make sure each of you always carries some food and water in case you ever get separated or lost.

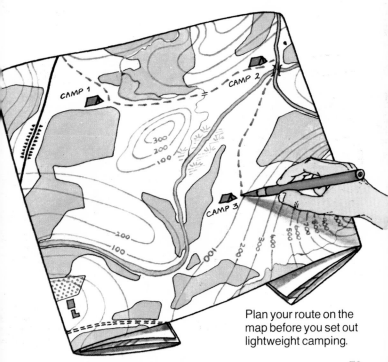

Plan your route on the map before you set out lightweight camping.

Clothing

What you need to take depends on where you go camping and the time of year. The pictures on the left page show some of the clothes you will need in cold and wet weather. Those on the right show some you need for hot, dry weather.

There are some clothes which you always need to take. These are: underwear,

Waterproof jacket with hood.
Jeans or **trousers,** two pairs.
Stout shoes; take walking boots if you intend to do a lot of walking.
Woolly socks, four pairs; wear two pairs with walking shoes.

Jumpers, two of medium thickness, and preferably made of wool.
Woolly hat; can be worn in bed if it is really cold.

take three of everything to allow for washing; a pair of lightweight canvas shoes, to wear in the tent; cotton T-shirts, to wear on their own when it is hot, or wear two or three under a jumper if cold; socks, woolly ones for walking boots, lighter ones for other shoes; jeans or trousers, two pairs in wet or cold weather, but only one if it is hot; jumpers, two for cold weather, and one in hot weather as nights can still be cold; waterproof jacket, the type shown here packs into a pocket and dries easily.

T-shirts, three; very useful in any weather and easy to wash. Wear at night to save taking pyjamas.
Shorts.
Sandals; good for messing about.
Sun hat; important in hot sun.

Swimwear; take two costumes or pairs of trunks if you are likely to do a lot of swimming.
Canvas shoes; wear them when messing about around camp.

Sleeping equipment

To keep warm and sleep comfortably outdoors you need protective covering underneath as well as over you, because the ground is usually much colder at night.

The best way to keep warm is to use a sleeping bag. There are many different types, but the main things to consider when buying one are filling, quilting and fastenings.

Simple quilting

Wall quilting

Filling is down or man-made fibre. The second is usually cheaper and washable, but bulkier. The type of quilting affects the warmth. "Simple quilting" with stitching right through the walls of the bag is not as warm as "wall quilting," which gives an even filling throughout. Fastenings are zip or drawstring. Zips give a cold spot unless lined.

How to make a blanket bag

You may find a blanket bag useful when you first start to camp. Although it is rather bulky, it is cheaper than buying a sleeping bag. To make one, you need three blankets and three blanket pins.

1

Fold blanket in half and turn up the bottom end.

2

Fold bottom blanket over top blanket.

3

Fold middle blanket over both the others.

4

Fold up the bottom ends of the blankets and secure with blanket pins.

How to make a sleeping bag container

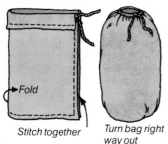

Fold

Stitch together

Turn bag right way out

If your sleeping bag is not sold with a container, you can either wrap it in a polythene bag or make a simple container as shown. Roll up your sleeping bag tightly and measure round it to find out how much material you need. Make sure you use waterproof material.

How to make a sheet lining bag

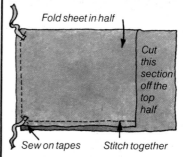

Fold sheet in half

Cut this section off the top half

Sew on tapes

Stitch together

A sheet liner will help to keep your sleeping bag clean inside. Make one from an old cotton sheet as shown. Sew tapes to the outside of the liner so that you can tie them with tapes in the bottom of your bag to stop the liner getting tangled round your feet.

Mattresses

A mattress makes sleeping on the ground more comfortable and is added protection against cold and damp.

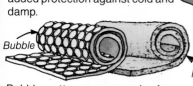

Bubble

Foam

Bubble mattresses are made of a double sheet of plastic with rows of air bubbles in the middle. They are cheap and light to carry. Foam mattresses are also very light.

Inflatable mattresses need a lot of "puff" to blow them up unless you use a pump. They are heavier than bubble or foam and you need a repair kit in case of a puncture.

If you need a mattress but have not taken one with you, try stuffing newspaper, leaves or grass under the groundsheet. Be careful not to include sticks, which could tear the groundsheet.

Preparation and packing

Once you have practised living outdoors overnight, you will have a good idea of what you need for camping. What you actually take with you on a camping trip will depend on where you are going and the time of year. Make a checklist of things to take by thinking about the journey there, any special hobbies or activities you are likely to take part in, and any personal gear you will need.

Check your tent and all your other equipment to make sure it is in working order and nothing is lost. Finally, make sure your parents know exactly where you are going. Write your address down for them in case they want to contact you while you are away.

Travelling

Put things you need for the journey, such as map, compass, food and drink, at the top of your pack so you can find them easily.

Activities

Pack any gear you need for a special hobby such as fishing. Take a camera if you have one and don't forget your swimming things.

Labelling

Label everything you are taking with you so you know it is yours. Paint initials on mug and plates, and tie cotton round cutlery.

Personal gear

Don't forget personal gear: money, pen and notebook or diary, books, glasses, and any tablets or other special medicines you need.

When it is time to pack, collect everything together and lay it in piles on the floor. Cross things off your checklist as you do so. Make sure your sleeping bag and mattress are rolled up as tightly as possible, and all your clothes are rolled neatly.

There are no strict rules for packing but here are a few tips. If you go with a friend, share out equipment such as the tent and cooking utensils into two equal piles. Pack everything in polythene bags to keep it dry. Roll clothing or towels up tightly and put inside billy cans. Try to keep the stove and fuel separate from everything else so there is no danger of spoiling food or staining clothes.

MAKE SURE THAT OBJECTS DO NOT STICK INTO YOUR BACK

Waterproof, map and food for journey handy in a pocket.

Tent and heavy objects at top and near your back.

Stove and fuel in separate pocket; all other things in middle of pack.

Sleeping bag and lighter things at the bottom.

Rucksacks

There is a bewildering assortment of rucksacks. Which one you choose will depend on what you want to use it for and how much you want to spend. Most rucksacks are made of nylon or canvas. They have one or two main compartments, and various pockets on the outside. One compartment is generally thought to be more versatile and easier to pack.

Remember that you should always walk upright when you are loaded with a pack. Leaning forward will give you backache.

Shoulder straps

Many packs are made for use without a frame, and they have shoulder straps for carrying them by. They tend to be smaller than packs with frames.

Frames

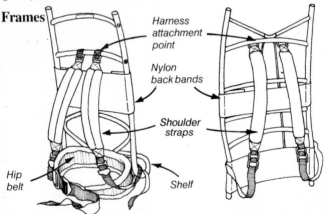

Harness attachment point

Nylon back bands

Shoulder straps

Hip belt

Shelf

Most larger packs are made so that they can be fixed onto frames of alloy tubing, which makes them easier to carry as the weight is better distributed. Frames have nylon back bands, and harnesses with wide padded shoulder straps. Some also have a hip belt, which may be padded. Some frames have a shelf at the bottom for carrying a sleeping mat or bag, or any other gear.

Buying a pack

Before you buy a pack, try it out with a load to see if it is comfortable. If you intend buying a pack with a frame, make sure nothing sticks into you or rubs against you. Remember that the larger the pack, the more you might be tempted to take with you. Check the points shown below to make sure that you are buying a reliable, well-made pack which will last.

1 Check the sac. Make sure all the seams are properly stitched and there is no sign of any frayed material. Check that all zips work.

2 Check that the frame is rigid. There should be no sharp edges and all the fixings should be secure.

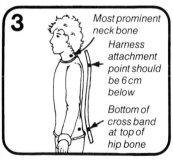

3
Most prominent neck bone

Harness attachment point should be 6 cm below

Bottom of cross band at top of hip bone

Check that the frame is the right size. If it is too long, it will rub against you and make you sore; if it is too short, it will put too much strain on your back as none of the weight will be carried on your hips. A good idea if you are still growing is to buy an adjustable frame.

TIP

Kitbag strapped to frame with belts

To save money, you can start with a pack that has a carrying harness, and buy a frame for it later on. Or you can start by buying a frame only, and making or buying something like a navy surplus kitbag to strap on.

Sleeping outdoors

If you go camping in warm, dry weather you can really enjoy the freedom of living outdoors and sleep without a tent. But remember that you will need a groundsheet under you, or a waterproofed sleeping bag, so that you do not get soaked by dew.

Bivouac shelters

If you prefer to have some protection over you, try using a large waterproof sheet to make a bivouac shelter. A sheet of thick polythene will do. It should be about 3 metres by $2\frac{1}{2}$ metres. Sew loops of tape onto the edges for pegging them to the ground.

Tents

Tents are essential for winter camping or if the weather is cold or wet. A tent provides privacy, shelter from bad weather or a hot sun, and protection from insects and inquisitive or hungry animals.

The simplest and cheapest tents are the ridge and the bell tents. They are both popular for standing and lightweight camps.

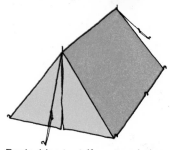

Basic ridge tent. If you touch the inside when it is raining it will leak, unless the material is coated.

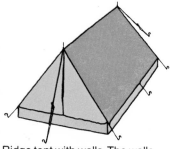

Ridge tent with walls. The walls give much more space around the edges of the tent.

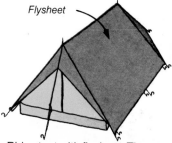

Flysheet

Ridge tent with flysheet. The flysheet helps to protect or insulate the tent from heat or cold, and stops rain leaking in.

Bell tent with single pole. This is light to carry but the pole takes up some of the space inside.

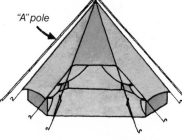

"A" pole

Bell tent with "A" pole. This has two poles on the outside instead of a single pole inside, so there is more space in the tent.

Choosing a tent

When choosing a tent you will have to think about the type you want, the materials it is made of, its size and weight, and whether any extras are included.

Study manufacturers' catalogues, then look around for any bargains in the shops: some tents are sold cheaply at the end of the season, or because they have been used as demonstration models.

The type of tent that you will probably find most useful is a ridge tent with a built-in groundsheet and a flysheet, like the one shown on this page. Do not make the mistake of getting a tent that is too heavy for you to carry. About 2.75 kilograms is a good weight for a two-person tent.

Fabric

Most tents are made of cotton or nylon. Cotton "breathes", so you do not get condensation inside the tent, but it is usually heavier and more expensive. It also stretches and shrinks with changes in the weather. Nylon tents are often cheaper, but nylon does not "breathe" as readily, so tents must have air vents.

Size

It is best to buy a two-person tent as you might want to share with a friend. Remember that your gear must fit inside the tent as well. A good size is 1.5 metres wide by two metres long and one metre high. You must be able to sit up and move around without touching the roof or walls.

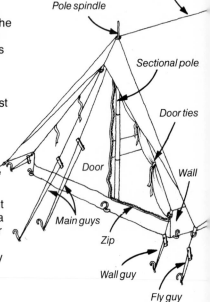

Ridge

Pole spindle

Sectional pole

Door ties

Door

Wall

Main guys

Zip

Wall guy

Fly guy

Colour

Tents are made in many different colours. Bright colours are easily seen from a distance and are often used in mountains, where mist and fog are a danger. In the

country, green or brown tents may be preferred, to blend with the scenery. Remember that a light colour will be brighter inside.

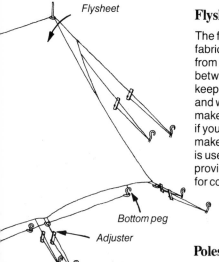

Flysheet

Bottom peg

Adjuster

Flysheet

The flysheet is an extra layer of fabric over the tent, held away from it so that there is a gap between the two layers. It helps to keep the tent cool in hot weather and warm in cold weather, and makes sure the tent does not leak if you touch it. You can also buy or make a flysheet extension, which is useful for storing equipment, providing a sheltered entrance, or for cooking in very bad weather.

Poles

Upright and ridge poles are usually made of wood, steel or metal alloy. Alloy is lightest and does not rust. Poles are in short sections which fit together; some pack inside one another to save space when carrying.

Groundsheet

Groundsheets are made in a variety of waterproof materials. If the groundsheet is built-in, it should extend at least 10 centimetres up the tent walls.

Setting up camp

When you arrive at your chosen camp site, you will have to decide exactly where to pitch your tent and which direction you want it to face.

Position your tent so that you have the most interesting view possible. If there is no obvious viewpoint, try pitching it so that you will be able to watch sunrise through the tent door. But be careful that the tent is not facing into strong wind, which could drive rain straight inside it.

If you are camping in summer, choose a place which catches the sun in the morning, but leaves the tent in the shade in the afternoon when you are likely to have had enough sun.

Once you have decided on the best position, go over the ground carefully. Remove any stones or twigs and stamp on any lumps.

If you do not bother to do this, you may regret it after a few nights of bad sleep, and you could even find holes in your groundsheet.

As soon as you have pitched the tent, fetch some drinking water. Set up and light your stove, and put some water on for a hot drink.

Unpack your sleeping bag and put it out to air. Put your spare shoes and the cooking utensils under the flysheet.

Set up a cooking area downwind from the tent and at least three metres away from it so there is no risk of fire. If you are using a stove,

choose or make a level place for it, so that pans do not slip off or fall over. Make sure it is sheltered from the wind.

Pitching a tent

Before you go camping, you should practise pitching your tent at home. Even if you are an experienced camper, you should practise if you have a new tent. A good idea is to put a sheet of polythene under the groundsheet. It protects the tent and keeps it clean.

The pictures on this page show how to pitch a ridge tent with two single poles and a built-in groundsheet. Those on the page opposite show how to pitch a ridge tent with two "A" poles and a separate groundsheet.

Pitching a ridge tent with built-in groundsheet

1

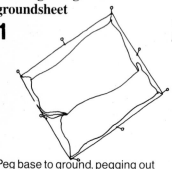

Peg base to ground, pegging out opposite corners first so that it is square and flat.

2

Straight ridge

Vertical poles

Close the doors

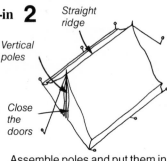

Assemble poles and put them in the spindle holes, rear one first. Lie them down and loosely peg out the main guys. Lift the poles upright and tighten the guys.

3

Wall guys should be about ⅔rds full length

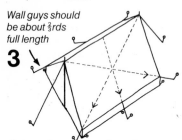

Peg each corner wall guy in a straight line from the opposite pole and each middle guy from the centre of the ridge. Adjust guys so tent is taut and square.

4

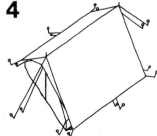

Place flysheet over tent, fitting holes over tent poles. Fix the main guys so the ridge is taut. Position pegs for side guys so flysheet is held away from tent.

Pitching a ridge tent with a separate groundsheet

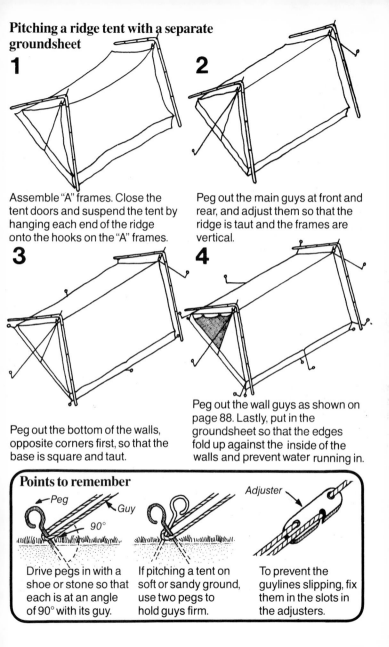

1

Assemble "A" frames. Close the tent doors and suspend the tent by hanging each end of the ridge onto the hooks on the "A" frames.

2

Peg out the main guys at front and rear, and adjust them so that the ridge is taut and the frames are vertical.

3

Peg out the bottom of the walls, opposite corners first, so that the base is square and taut.

4

Peg out the wall guys as shown on page 88. Lastly, put in the groundsheet so that the edges fold up against the inside of the walls and prevent water running in.

Points to remember

Drive pegs in with a shoe or stone so that each is at an angle of 90° with its guy.

If pitching a tent on soft or sandy ground, use two pegs to hold guys firm.

To prevent the guylines slipping, fix them in the slots in the adjusters.

Running a camp

Standing camps need some organization if they are to be enjoyed and the site left unscarred at the end of the camp. Apart from adequate supplies of food and water, you will have to think about washing your clothes and disposing of rubbish, and you will need to organize a toilet area. If you adopt a daily routine for basic essentials, they will take up very little time.

Prepare a menu before you go. If you plan ahead, you should only need to go shopping about every four days.

In fine weather, air the tent during the day by tying the doors back. Hang sleeping bags over the tent or a tree to air them too.

1 Rubbish

Keep rubbish in a polythene bag. Tie the bag to a tent guy or a tree near your cooking area so inquisitive animals can't get it.

Flatten empty cans by stamping on them so that they will take up less space in the rubbish bag.

If you have a fire you can burn most rubbish. Greasy water should be strained through bracken or grass, which can then be burnt.

BE ESPECIALLY CAREFUL WITH PLASTICS, ALUMINIUM FOIL AND GLASS, WHICH WON'T DECAY IF LEFT LYING AROUND. THEY ARE A DANGER TO ANIMALS, AND GLASS CAN START FIRES

How to make a toilet

To make a toilet you need to select a private place where you can dig a hole about half a metre deep. Pile the loose earth on one side and keep a trowel by it, so that each time the toilet is used some of the earth can be scattered back. Keep toilet paper in a polythene bag to keep it dry.

Washing clothes

Use separate bags for clean and dirty clothes. The dirty clothes bag can be kept under the flysheet. When you wash clothes, hang them out to dry on bushes or trees, or use string to make a washing line. If you use a double length of twisted string, you can tuck your washing into it and make do without pegs.

In general, wash clothes only when the weather is good, but if you are doing a lot of walking, wash your socks every day.

Washing

You may think that because you have the minimum of equipment and facilities at camp, it is a good opportunity to forget about such things as washing and bathing. Far from it! Since you will probably be involved in more strenuous activities than normal, washing is particularly important.

Do not waste drinking water by using it for washing, unless there is a plentiful supply. Take your washing gear to the nearest water source: a tap, river or lake, and wash there. It saves carrying water back to the tent. Do remember to use drinking water for cleaning your teeth.

Always wash your hands before handling food or preparing a meal, and after using the toilet.

Have a good all-over wash every three or four days and shampoo your hair at the same time. Make your own bath at camp if there is no lake or river nearby: dig a shallow hole and line it with a piece of polythene.

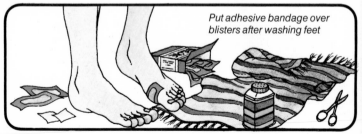

Put adhesive bandage over blisters after washing feet

Hardworking feet must be looked after carefully. Wash them thoroughly every day and dry well, especially between the toes. Use foot powder generously. Trim your toe nails regularly.

Flannel

Always rinse out your flannel after use, then put it out to dry on a bush, stone or stick. If it becomes smelly, you can boil it.

Soap

Keep soap dry in a container, otherwise you will end up with a slimy mess. If you put it down on the ground it will get covered with earth or grass.

Wash bag

Foot powder

Small plastic bottle of shampoo

Comb

Towel

Take a small towel rather than a bath size one. It will dry more quickly and will take up less room in your pack.
Always hang it up to dry after use, but take it into the tent at night to prevent it getting damp with dew.

Toothbrush

If you forget to take your toothbrush or toothpaste with you, you can use your finger instead. Dip it in salt in place of toothpaste.

Cooking equipment

The equipment shown on this page is the minimum for two or three campers eating fresh cooked food. If you go lightweight camping, you will probably eat mostly dried, prepacked food and need less equipment.

Basic gear

Use a plate as a lid if you need one

Bottle opener on handle

Billy cans

You need two which fit or "nest" inside each other. They should be big enough to make a stew in and should be wide rather than deep.

Pan holder

Allows you to grip pans firmly without getting burnt. It can be carried inside billy cans.

Frying pan

Preferably non-stick with a folding handle, and the right size to fit on top of one of the billy cans so it can be used as a lid.

Wooden spatula

This will not scratch the frying pan. It can also be used for stirring and serving.

Can opener

A large one like this is best. It is easier to use and safer than the small ones, which leave ragged edges on tins.

Water bottle

Take a collapsible bottle big enough to hold $4\frac{1}{2}$ litres of water. The ones that have a flat base and can stand up are the easiest to fill.

Useful extras

Chopping board

A piece of plywood about 12 centimetres square is invaluable for cutting up vegetables.

Sharp knife

One about 15 centimetres long will make cutting bread and vegetables much easier.

Plastic strainer

Plastic is best because the flexible mesh makes it easier to pack. Use it for straining noodles, spaghetti, rice, tea and vegetables.

Plastic bowl with lid

Useful for mixing omelettes and pancake batter. Choose one that will fit inside your billy cans, and use it to keep food in while travelling.

Wire whisk

Saves time when making pancake batter and omelettes, and can be used to beat unwanted lumps out of things.

Personal gear

Label plates and cutlery

These are the things you will need for eating. Plastic is best as it does not chip or break.

Use plates to prepare food on as well as for eating, and use your mug for measuring.

Stoves

Cooking in the open air is fun, especially on a wood fire. But you may sometimes camp where there is no wood for fuel or where you are not allowed to light fires. Then you will need a stove to cook on.

There are many camping stoves to choose from. Different stoves use different kinds of fuel, so your choice will depend partly on the cost and availability of fuel. The type of camp will also help to decide which stove you should choose. Weight is most important for light-weight camping but the running cost could be a more important factor in standing camps.

Types of stove

The most popular types of stove use butane gas or paraffin, but there are also stoves that use petrol, methylated spirits or special tablets of solid fuel.

Solid fuel stoves are small and lightweight, but they do not give out as much heat as the others and are not very good for cooking. Their main purpose is for heating soup and hot drinks when you are out on day hikes.

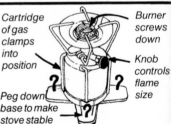

Cartridge of gas clamps into position

Burner screws down

Knob controls flame size

Peg down base to make stove stable

Gas cartridge stoves are good for lightweight camping as you do not need to carry a separate fuel container or funnel. The throw-away cartridge makes the stove easy to use but expensive.

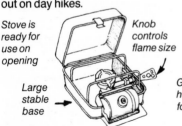

Stove is ready for use on opening

Knob controls flame size

Large stable base

Petrol stoves must be handled with care as the fuel can be dangerous. This stove is easy to use and folds away neatly, but petrol is an expensive fuel.

Grip handle for pans

This **methylated spirit stove** is excellent for lightweight camping as it is a complete cooking set which packs into a small space and is light to carry.

How to use a paraffin pressure stove

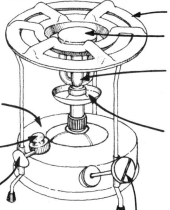

Top ring

Burner

1. *Fill* **tank** *with fuel (not more than ¾ full)*

2. *Close* **filler cap** *tightly*

3. *Open* **air valve**

4. *Prick* **jet** *to clean it, so that paraffin vapour can escape*

5. *Put priming fuel in* **priming tray** *and light it*

6. *Close* **air valve** *when fuel is almost burnt out*

7. *Give* **pressure pump** *one or two slow pumps: a small blue flame should appear on burner as paraffin vapour catches alight. Give a few harder pumps*

Paraffin pressure stoves are the cheapest to run, but they need a second fuel, known as the primer, to start them working. The primer (methylated spirits or solid fuel) is used to quickly heat up the burner so that it is hot enough to vaporize the paraffin pumped up from the tank. The paraffin vapour burns and provides the heat for cooking.

If you pump too fast when you first light the stove, a sooty yellow flame will appear; liquid paraffin is being forced into the burner before it can vaporize. Turn off at once by opening the valve. Put more priming fuel in the tray and try again.

DO'S....

DO READ AND FOLLOW INSTRUCTIONS

DO KEEP FUEL AWAY FROM LIGHTED STOVE

....& DON'TS

DON'T COOK NEAR TENT. IT MIGHT CATCH FIRE

DO KEEP MATCHES IN A WATERPROOF TIN OR BOTTLE

DO CARRY FUEL IN A POLYTHENE BOTTLE. TAKE A FUNNEL

DON'T LEAVE EMPTY GAS CONTAINERS LYING AROUND, OR NEAR A FIRE – THEY MIGHT EXPLODE

Camp fires

REMEMBER! ALWAYS GET PERMISSION FROM LANDOWNER BEFORE MAKING A FIRE

DO'S....

DO POSITION DOWNWIND, 3 METRES FROM TENT

DO CLEAR ANYTHING THAT MIGHT CATCH FIRE

DO COLLECT ENOUGH WOOD BEFORE YOU START

DO KEEP WATER OR A STICK HANDY TO PUT OUT FIRE

DO MAKE SURE YOU PUT OUT FIRE AFTER USE

....& DON'TS

DON'T PUT UPWIND FROM TENT, OR IN A WINDY PLACE

DON'T POSITION UNDER BUSHES OR TREES – THEY MAY CATCH FIRE

DON'T POSITION ON LEAF MOULD OR THICK PINE NEEDLES

DON'T EVER LEAVE A FIRE UNATTENDED

Preparing the ground

1. On grass

Cut out turf. Try to keep each piece whole by rolling it back.

2.

Store turf flat. Put it upside down in a cool damp place.

3.

Line edges of hole with logs or stones to protect grass.

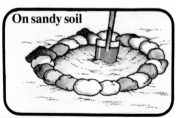

On sandy soil

Dig a shallow pit and surround it with stones. Do not use flint or river stones, they can explode.

On wet ground

Make a bed of stones, sand or green sticks, which don't burn readily, to build your fire on.

Search trees and bushes for dead twigs and branches, which are leafless and break off easily. This wood is dry and burns well. Dead wood from the ground is often too damp to burn. See page 129.

If the sticks you collect are too long for use, break them up as shown. Nick each stick on opposite sides with a penknife, and then snap it sharply over a log or rock at the nicked point, using your foot.

Laying a fire

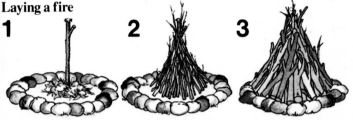

1 **2** **3**

Start by pushing a forked stick into the ground in the centre of your fireplace. Add dry grass, lightly crumpled paper or a strip of birch bark around it and then build up a tent of dry twigs, gradually increasing their size.

If you have a very big log, build a fire around the middle of it and push the ends in as it burns. You can also do this with two logs, one leant over the other.

TIP

If you do not have paper, bark or dry grass for a fire, cut shavings on a dry stick. Use this as your central fire stick, building a tent of twigs around it.

Supporting your cooking pan

A well-built fire is one in which the outside wood keeps falling into the burning centre. The fire is continually being refuelled, and any wood that is slightly damp will dry out first on the outside.

Fires built for cooking do not need to be big. Large fires waste fuel and are more difficult to put out when you have finished using them. The pictures below show several ways to cook over a fire.

Use two large logs or stones and rest two metal bars or green sticks across them to support your pan. Place a piece of metal mesh over the logs for barbecuing.

Dig a pit for a trench fire and rest your billy on the edges. The pit should slope down to a depth of about 20 centimetres at one end, for the fire. Lay the fuel lengthwise.

Hang a billy over the fire on a notched stick, supported by a crossbar and forked sticks placed either side of the fire, as shown.

Build a fire around two flat stones on which you can then rest your billy.

Hang a billy from a stick held in place by stones as shown.

Or raise the stick over the fire by using two other forked sticks.

Food and storage

Eat on day of purchase

Fresh meat and fish should always be cooked and eaten on the day they are bought. If you buy frozen food you will need to eat it the same day.

Eat within a few days

Bacon and other meat containing preservatives can be kept a bit longer. Eggs and cheese, and fresh fruit and vegetables will also keep for several days.

Keep as long as you like

Many foods can be kept almost indefinitely. Take the following with you: flour, sugar, breakfast cereal, tea, coffee, squash, herbs, salt and pepper, and cooking oil. Also take with you as much of the following as you have room for: canned meat and fish; dried foods such as rice, pasta, lentils, fruit and nuts, and milk powder; packet sauce mixes and soup, and freeze-dried vegetables.

Storing food

Stones

Billy can

Try these ideas to keep food fresh, and safe from insects and animals. Keep fruit and vegetables in a string bag hung from a tree. Dig a hole in the ground for food such as cheese and sausages; cover it with greenery, and leave a sign so no-one steps in it. Stand milk in water with a damp cloth over. If there is a stream near, put food in a plastic bag tied to the bank.

Cooking on a stove

1 Wind wastes a lot of heat. Make a shield of sticks or stones to protect your stove, or use a bag stretched over two sticks in the ground. See also page 119.

2 Before you start cooking, plan the best order of preparation for a meal. Remember that you only have one stove, two billies, and a frying pan.

3 Meat and vegetables cook more quickly if cut up small. Cook all the vegetables for a meal together in one billy.

Cover billy with a cloth

4 Begin by half-cooking vegetables, pasta or rice. Keep them warm and they will be ready by the time the sauce or meat is cooked.

Rice and vegetable salad

5 Cook extra helpings of vegetables, noodles or rice. Eat them the next day with a sauce, as a salad, or fried.

6 Whenever the stove is alight but not being used to cook, such as between two courses of a meal, use it to boil water for washing up or a hot drink afterwards.

Sterilizing water

If you can't get tap water, you must sterilize water before using it for cooking or drinking. Filter it through cloth or two layers of nylon stocking until clear, then boil it or use purifying tablets. If using tablets, you need to add special tablets afterwards to improve the taste.

A filling meal for two people

This page shows how to plan and cook a filling meal for two people. The menu is: soup, noodles with tomato sauce, and pancakes. You will need:

For the soup: a half litre packet of soup.

For the main course: 200 grams of pasta; a small tin of tomato puree; an onion; a mug of milk (can be made from milk powder); 3 tablespoons of oil or butter; pinch of salt and pepper.

For the pancakes: an egg; 3 tablespoons of flour; a mug of milk; small amount of margarine; pinch of salt; jam, or lemon and sugar to put on cooked pancakes.

Light stove. Put on large billy full of water. Cover.

Mix flour, egg and salt. Add milk slowly. Beat to smooth batter.

Use some of the hot water to make soup in second billy.

While soup is cooking, chop up onion. Open tin of tomato puree.

Drink soup. Boil water left in first billy. Add pasta and salt.

Take half-cooked pasta off stove. Fry onion in oil in soup billy.

Add milk, tomato puree, salt and pepper. Stir until sauce is hot.

Test pasta by cutting. If hard inside, cook a little longer.

Drain pasta. Serve with sauce and eat.

Heat a teaspoon of margarine in frying pan. Pour in ½ cup of batter.

Cook for about a minute. Turn over when underside is golden.

When cooked on both sides, eat with lemon juice and sugar, or jam.

Camp fire cooking

Food cooked over a camp fire has a delicious flavour. You must let the fire burn down to red coals before you start cooking; flames only burn and blacken food. If you are going to use a fire for grilling, you will need green sticks for cooking utensils. Food can also be cooked in the ashes. It is usually best wrapped in aluminium foil to keep in the flavour and juices.

Cooking on sticks

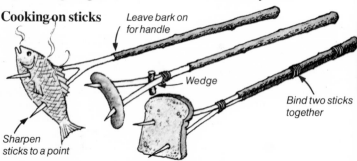

Leave bark on for handle

Wedge

Bind two sticks together

Sharpen sticks to a point

Cook fish, sausages and toast on sticks of green wood with the bark stripped off. Use forked sticks so the food does not drop off into the fire. If you can't find a forked stick, make one by splitting a large stick for part of its length and wedging it open with a piece of wood. Or bind two sticks together at one end.

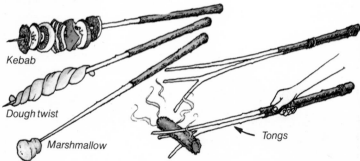

Kebab

Dough twist

Marshmallow

Tongs

Marshmallows, kebabs and twists can be cooked on straight sticks. Make twists by adding water to a mug of flour to make a stiff dough. Toast on a stick. Fill with jam to eat.

Tongs are useful for picking up stray embers and any food that falls off sticks while cooking. Make them from green wood, by lashing together forked and curved sticks.

Cooking in foil in the ashes

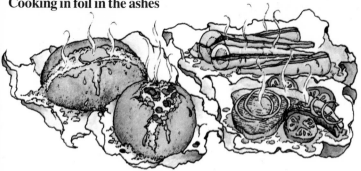

Potatoes Scrub, wrap in foil and bury in hot ashes for half an hour to an hour, depending on size. Eat with butter or cheese.

Apples Cut out core and fill the centre with currants and sugar. Wrap in foil and bury in ashes for 25-45 minutes.

Parsnips Peel or scrub, and cut into "sticks". Wrap up in foil, dotting with butter as you do so, and cook in ashes for 30-40 minutes.

Chops and **steaks** Wrap in foil with tomato and mushrooms and a pinch of salt, and bury in ashes for 30 minutes.

More methods

Heat a flat stone in the fire until it is nearly red hot. Dust any ash off it, brush with oil and use to cook meat and fish on.

Make a barbecue by supporting a piece of metal mesh on logs over hot coals. Brush the mesh with oil before you put food on it.

To cook an egg, prick a hole in one end and stand in hot ashes for ten minutes. Or, cut the top off an orange, scoop out the flesh and cook egg in "shell".

Cook a stew overnight in a billy stood in hot ashes. Make sure you cover the billy with a lid or plate and bank the ashes up round it almost to the top. Boil up the next day before eating.

Clearing up after a meal

After eating, close all food containers and put them back in their place so you will know where to find them again. Dispose of rubbish, as shown on page 90, so it does not attract insects or become a danger to animals. Collect dirty dishes together and have plenty of hot water ready for washing them.

Wipe your plate with bread when you finish a meal. It will fill you up if you are still hungry, and make washing up easier.

Dishes become more difficult to clean if they are left standing, so wash up straight away. Use the largest billy to wash up in.

Dishcloth — Brush — Washing up liquid in plastic bottle — Pan scourer — Washing soda crystals

You will need the items shown above for washing up, but don't use the scourer on non-stick pans. You may find washing soda crystals more convenient to use than liquid, as a small quantity can be kept in a plastic bag and you only need one spoonful at a time.

Dry everything with a tea towel. Start with the plates so that other things can be stacked on top as shown here.

When you finish, hang tea towels out to dry. Put things away so that they are always in the same place and can be found again.

How to put out a fire

If you cook on a fire, use dirty washing up water to put it out. Sprinkle water over fire with your fingers.

Then use a green stick to spread out the smouldering embers a little, so they will cool off more quickly.

Sprinkle more water onto the remains of the fire. Do not leave it until you are quite sure it is out.

Things to make

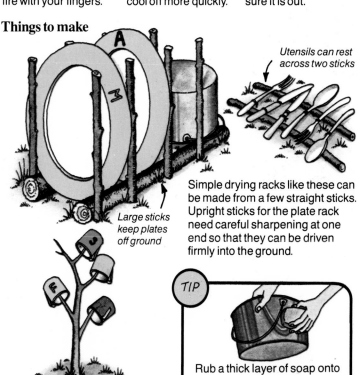

Utensils can rest across two sticks

Large sticks keep plates off ground

Simple drying racks like these can be made from a few straight sticks. Upright sticks for the plate rack need careful sharpening at one end so that they can be driven firmly into the ground.

Mugs can be kept on a "mug tree". Choose a strong, branched stick and push it into the ground so that it stands firmly upright.

TIP

Rub a thick layer of soap onto the outside of billy cans before you use them for cooking. It makes them much easier to wash clean after use.

Things to do

July 12th
Sunny and quite warm.
Cornflakes, sausages + bacon for breakfast

Did some tracking in the woods. Found a Pheasant's feather, part of the shell of a thrush's egg, and saw these footprints

Squirrel footprints

Bread, cheese, salad + fruit for lunch. Played football in a field nearby, and found this butterfly wing

Red Admiral Butterfly wing

Went into Bray village – lovely old houses and shops. (this is part of a postcard)

Risotto for supper. Played cards.

Whenever you go camping, it is interesting and useful to keep a diary. You will have hours of fun looking back over it long after the camp has ended. A hard-backed notebook is best. Get into the habit of writing in it every evening, and make sketches too. Note down the weather, the food you have eaten, where you went and the route you followed, and what you saw. Anything new you found out or want to find out more about should also be included.

In bad weather

Take with you some playing cards, a pocket chess or draughts set, dice, books, and a selection of pencils, colouring pens and paper.

Use the time to clean and repair clothes and equipment. Then try inventing and making new gadgets which might be useful at camp.

During the day

Get up early to watch the sun rise. Animals are more likely to be seen earlier too, especially near water where they go to drink.

Look for animal tracks, and signs such as burrows, droppings, hair or feathers. Collect seashells or leaves, but do not pick flowers.

If you get tired of games such as football, try competitions such as seeing who can skim a small stone furthest across the sea or a lake.

Try tracking: one person sets off 20 minutes before the others and leaves a trail for them to follow. Use signs such as those above.

At night

Go for a night walk. Keep quiet so that you will hear any noises made by animals that are active at night. Try spotting stars.

WARNING! USE A TORCH IN THE TENT, NOT A CANDLE, THE TENT MIGHT CATCH FIRE

Sit round a camp fire and sing, tell stories or play charades. Discuss and plan what to do and where to go the next day.

Striking camp

When it is time to go home or move onto another site, you will have to dismantle your camp, pack, and clear up the site. This is known as "striking camp". It is best to follow the routine shown here, packing first and taking down the tent last. This way you will still keep fairly dry if it rains while you are striking camp.

After your last meal, wash up and prepare food and drink for the journey. If you used a stove, leave it to cool, then empty and clean it.

Collect all your things together outside the tent, or inside if it is wet. Check them against your list to see that you have everything.

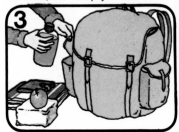

Pack everything. Put tickets, food, drink, money, maps, jacket and anything else you may need on the journey at the top or in pockets.

When you have packed everything except the tent, clear up the site. Pick up any remaining rubbish and burn it or put it in the farmer's dustbin. If you can't do

either of these, bury it or take it home. Fill in any holes you made for a fireplace or toilet. If turf was removed, replace it, stamp it down and water thoroughly.

Sweep out the tent. Take it down by reversing the order of the stages you followed for pitching it.

Make sure you pull up all the pegs. In hard ground, you may need to use a piece of string as shown, or a peg puller (see page 117).

Fold up guy ropes carefully and tie each one in a large knot so that they do not get tangled.

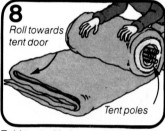

Roll towards tent door

Tent poles

Fold tent with the groundsheet outside and wipe over. Fold up the flysheet and lay on top. Dismantle poles and roll tent up round them, rolling towards the tent entrance so that no air is trapped inside.

9

Always leave a site exactly as you found it. Take a last look round to make sure nothing is left behind; you will be surprised at how often you discover an odd piece of washing.

Arriving home

As soon as possible after arriving home, check over all your equipment and clothing. When you unpack, put things you have not used in a separate pile and see if there is anything you need not take next time. When you have done this, make a new check-list of equipment. Include on it anything you needed but did not take.

Wash or air your sleeping bag and then store it lightly folded. Make sure all your clothes are washed, and your sleeping bag liner if you used one.

Clean your shoes or walking boots. Brush or scrape dirt off them, then treat with boot oil or wax, rubbing it in with an old cloth.

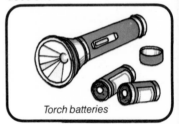

Torch batteries

If you do not use your torch at home, take the batteries out before putting it away so that they do not rot it.

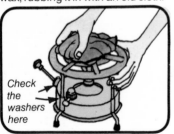

Check the washers here

If you used a stove, make sure no fuel is left in it, then clean and polish it. Look for signs of wear and replace parts such as washers if necessary.

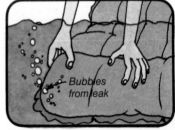

Bubbles from leak

If you have an air mattress, check that it has not sprung a leak by dipping it, a bit at a time, in a bath or basin of water. Look for bubbles which show where there is a hole.

Air your tent to make sure it is dry. Wipe pole joints with an oily cloth and clean pegs, straightening any that are bent. Check your tent and rucksack for signs of wear.

When you have finished cleaning and repairing your equipment, put it all together in a box and store in a dry place. You can then find it easily when you want it again.

Repairs

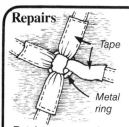

Tape

Metal ring

Patch tears round the spindle holes by pushing lengths of tape through the metal ring and stitching both sides.

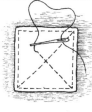

Mend a tear in the tent wall with a square of fabric, larger than the tear. Turn the edges under and sew on.

"D" ring

If a guy is torn off, patch the tear, then sew a tape round with a metal "D" ring on it, to which the guy can be attached.

A hole in the groundsheet can be patched underneath with adhesive carpet tape, or by using a bicycle puncture kit.

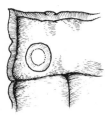

A bicycle puncture kit is also useful for repairing a hole in your air mattress.

If you use the tent a lot, you should treat it every year with waterproofing agent, which you can buy in a spray can.

Weather

The site you choose for pitching your tent, the food you eat and the way you store it, the clothes you wear and your daily camp routine all depend on the weather. These pages show some tips and points to remember for camping in different kinds of weather.

Hot weather

If it is very hot you could sleep in the open instead of in your tent. You might find it more comfortable in a hammock.

Pitch your tent in shade, if possible in a position where it will catch any breeze. Keep tent doors and any air vents open.

Hot weather is much more tiring. If it is very hot, take salt tablets with you. Remember to take calamine lotion too, in case of sunburn.

Keeping food fresh is much more difficult in hot weather. If there is a stream near the camp, you can use it as a larder (see page 101).

Wet weather

Tents without flysheets are likely to leak if touched inside. You can stop leaks by dripping candle wax onto the leak on the outside.

Pitch your tent on the highest ground available so that water will drain away from your site and not towards it.

Wear sandals and shorts rather than shoes, socks and trousers. You will be more comfortable if you get soaked.

Always pack all your equipment in plastic bags so that, even if the tent leaks, your things will not get wet.

If the groundsheet is not built-in, it is a good idea to fold it back from the door so it does not get wet and muddy.

If it rains so much that water starts to run under the tent, dig a small trench around it on three sides to drain the water away. Make sure you fill the trench in before leaving the site.

Cold weather

Pitch your tent on a site sheltered from the wind. Keep the doors and air vents closed.

In extremely cold weather, a sleeping bag liner can be filled with dry leaves or hay and used as a mattress or a cover. The ground gets much colder at night, so you need plenty of protection under as well as over you.

Keep warm at night by wearing more clothes. Socks, underwear, a pullover and even a woolly hat will keep you warm in bed.

Build a reflector fire

If it is very cold, open the tent doors and build a reflector fire about a metre in front of the tent. This kind of fire is built with a barrier behind it so that heat is reflected in one direction, in this case, towards the tent. The barrier is usually a small wall of logs, but almost any large flat object will do. See page 100 for how to make a fire safely.

Extra tips

If you are pitching your tent on sandy soil, bury the tent pegs in the soil, so they are anchored as firmly as possible.

Tent pegs are quite easy to make. Find a forked stick and shave one end off to a point so it can be driven into the ground.

Boots are best kept outside the tent to air them. Put them upside down on sticks like this, so air can circulate all round.

When you use a forked stick to make a camp gadget, choose one like A, which can be driven into the ground easily. Fork B will be no use, it will probably split.

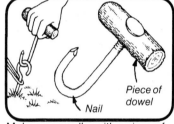

Make a peg puller with a piece of wood, dowel is ideal, and a long nail. Drill a hole in the wood, then push the nail through and bend it with a pair of pliers.

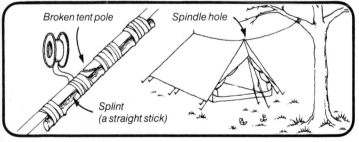

If a tent pole breaks, bind it firmly to a splint with string or tape from a first aid kit. Or use string to hang the tent from a tree: thread one end of the string down through the spindle hole and tie it round a small object such as a peg. Tie the other end up to the tree.

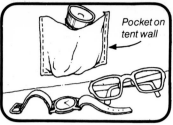

A pocket sewn on to the tent wall is useful for keeping a pair of glasses, a watch, or a torch handy. It should be made of a similar fabric to the tent.

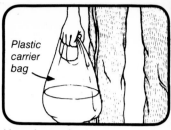

Use a large plastic carrier bag as an extra water carrier. Check the bag over first to make sure it is not the type with holes in. Never fill it more than half full.

If you are caught in the rain without a waterproof jacket, you can use a large polythene bag. Cut a narrow hole along the bottom edge of the bag near one end, and wear this end over your head.

Take an old pillow case with you to make a pillow. You can stuff it with spare clothing, such as jumpers and T-shirts, or anything else you can find like leaves, grass or straw.

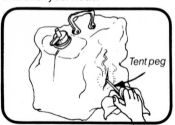

You can seal a hole in a polythene container such as a water carrier by using a tent peg. Heat the peg until it is hot enough to melt the polythene, then smear it across the hole. Hold the hot peg with a cloth.

A magnifying glass can be used to light a camp fire on a clear sunny day if you run out of matches. Hold it at an angle so that it catches the sun's rays and directs them onto kindling in a fireplace.

An extra cooking pot can be made from a large can. Punch two holes just below the rim and thread wire through for a handle.

If you collect wood for a fire, stack it under a bush or up against a tree. If it rains, the wood will stay dry.

Make a wind shield for cooking from four bicycle spokes or pieces of garden cane, and a strip of fabric one metre long. See also page 102.

Emergency kit

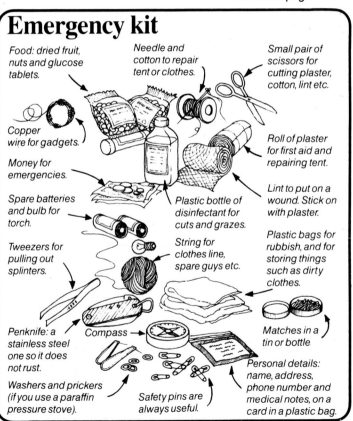

Food: dried fruit, nuts and glucose tablets.

Needle and cotton to repair tent or clothes.

Small pair of scissors for cutting plaster, cotton, lint etc.

Copper wire for gadgets.

Money for emergencies.

Roll of plaster for first aid and repairing tent.

Spare batteries and bulb for torch.

Plastic bottle of disinfectant for cuts and grazes.

Lint to put on a wound. Stick on with plaster.

Tweezers for pulling out splinters.

String for clothes line, spare guys etc.

Plastic bags for rubbish, and for storing things such as dirty clothes.

Penknife: a stainless steel one so it does not rust.

Compass

Matches in a tin or bottle.

Washers and prickers (if you use a paraffin pressure stove).

Safety pins are always useful.

Personal details: name, address, phone number and medical notes, on a card in a plastic bag.

Recipes

Plan your menu so that you have a good breakfast and evening meal. Sandwiches or salad will do midday. Try the following ideas:
Breakfast. Cereal or muesli; scrambled, boiled or fried egg with fried bacon and tomato; fried or eggy bread; kipper; sausages.

Midday. Salad; sandwiches with cheese, sausage, paté, hard-boiled egg, jam, cold meat, sardines, or tuna; crisps; dried fruit and nuts.
Evening meal. Soup; curry and rice; omelette; stew with dumplings; risotto; kebabs; pasta with sauce; rice salad; beefburgers; fruit or jelly.

Muesli (for one person)

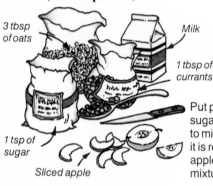

3 tbsp of oats

Milk

1 tbsp of currants

1 tsp of sugar

Sliced apple

Put porridge oats, currants and sugar in a mug or bowl. Stir round to mix up, then add some milk and it is ready to eat. Try adding sliced apple and nuts to the muesli mixture as well.

Eggy bread (for two)

1 tbsp of cooking oil

1 tbsp of milk

4 slices of bread

Pinch of salt and pepper

3 eggs

Mix eggs, milk, salt and pepper together in a billy. Put the bread in this mixture and leave it to soak for a few minutes. Heat the cooking oil in the frying pan and fry each slice of bread on both sides until it is golden brown.

Omelette (for two)

1 tbsp of oil

3 tbsp milk

4 eggs

Salt and pepper

Omelette fillings

Mix eggs, milk, salt and pepper in a mug with a fork. Heat the oil in the frying pan, pour in half the mixture and cook until set. Fold in half to serve. Try filling the omelette with ham, cheese, mushrooms or any other cooked vegetables.

Beefburgers (for two)

Pinch of salt and pepper

250 grams of minced beef

Medium onion

One egg

One slice of bread

Beat the egg in a bowl and add the slice of bread to soak it up. Chop the onion finely, then mix it thoroughly with the minced beef, salt and pepper, and egg-soaked bread. Divide mixture in two, roll into balls and flatten. Fry burgers for about ten minutes each side.

Macaroni cheese (for two)

Large mugful of macaroni

Packet of cheese sauce mix

2 tomatoes, sliced

Grated cheese

Cook the macaroni in boiling salted water for ten minutes, until it is soft. Make up the cheese sauce, following the instructions on the packet. Drain the macaroni and mix it into the sauce. Top with tomato and cheese to serve.

Rice salad (for two)

Mug of rice

4 tbsp of oil

1 tbsp of currants

Pinch of salt and pepper

Juice of a lemon

Small onion

Chopped vegetables

Handful of peanuts

Cook rice in a large billy of boiling salted water for about fifteen minutes, until just soft. Drain and leave to go cold. Chop up or grate small quantities of any vegetables available and add to cold rice. Mix together the oil, lemon juice, salt and pepper in a mug. Pour over the salad and mix carefully with a spoon handle to keep the ingredients whole.

Potato curry (for two)

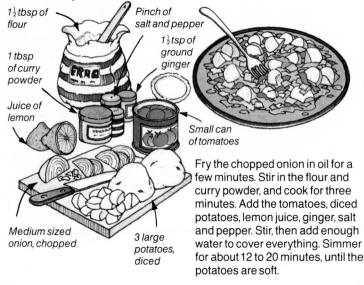

$1\frac{1}{2}$ tbsp of flour

Pinch of salt and pepper

$1\frac{1}{2}$ tsp of ground ginger

1 tbsp of curry powder

Juice of lemon

Small can of tomatoes

Medium sized onion, chopped

3 large potatoes, diced

Fry the chopped onion in oil for a few minutes. Stir in the flour and curry powder, and cook for three minutes. Add the tomatoes, diced potatoes, lemon juice, ginger, salt and pepper. Stir, then add enough water to cover everything. Simmer for about 12 to 20 minutes, until the potatoes are soft.

Instant stew (for two)

Can of meat

Packet of dried vegetables (or left-overs)

Large packet of vegetable soup

Dumplings

3 tbsp of flour

Large potato (200 grams) peeled and cut up

Pinch of salt

Make up the vegetable soup, following the instructions on the packet. Add the canned meat and the vegetables, and cook together. To make the dumplings, first boil the potatoes until soft, then mash them. Mix together with the flour and salt until you get a thick paste. Roll into small balls, dip in flour and drop into boiling stew. Cook for about ten minutes.

Risotto (for two)

$\frac{1}{2}$ mug of rice

$\frac{1}{2}$ packet of soup

Mug of water

1 tbsp of oil

1 tbsp of butter

100 grams of mushrooms, sliced

2 tomatoes, sliced (or small can)

Medium onion

Heat oil and butter together in the frying pan and fry rice until golden brown. Add chopped onion and fry for a few minutes. Then add mushrooms and tomatoes. Mix the packet soup with cold water and add to the rice and vegetables. Cook, stirring gently, until the rice has absorbed all the liquid.

Knots

There are a great variety of knots, designed for all sorts of different purposes. These pages show only a few of the many you will come across.

All of them are knots which might be useful when you are camping, either for mending things or for making camp gadgets.

Clove hitch

This is a good knot for tying something to a post or pole.

 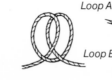

Loop A

Loop B

Make two loops like this.

Place loop A over loop B.

Slip the loops over the post.

Pull both ends of rope tightly.

Heaving line bend

Use this knot for tying together two ropes of different thickness.

Sling

This is the best way to carry a can or bucket without a handle.

Place the can on the string.

Tie the ends of the string over each other on top.

Pull tie apart and slip over edges of can.

Tighten string round can and tie ends for handle.

Whipping

This is used for binding things together firmly and neatly. You might use it on a loose knife handle.

Loop

1

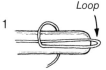

Place cord round object, making a long loop as shown above.

2

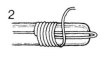

Bind cord neatly round and round, working from left to right.

3

When you have finished, put the end of the cord through the loop.

4

Pull on the end of the cord labelled B.

5

This pulls the other end under the binding.

6

Cut off the remaining ends of the cord.

How to make a rope ladder

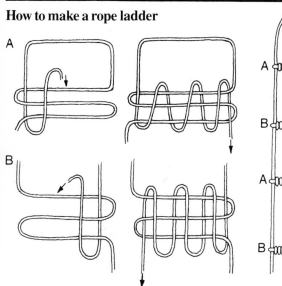

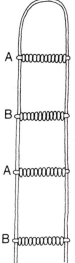

Sheepshank

This is used to shorten a rope or to strengthen a frayed or worn section in the middle of a rope.

Make a double bend in the rope like the letter "z". Each of these bends is known as a "bight".

Make a loop in the lower of the two free ends as shown. Slip it over the upper bight and pull it tight.

Repeat to fix a loop over the lower bight. If the knot is correct, it will get tighter as you pull the free ends harder.

Slippery hitch

Use this knot to tie something to a post. It will not slip, but can be released quickly if required.

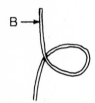 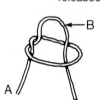 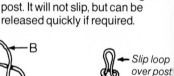

Make a loop near one end of the rope as shown. The end of the rope is labelled B in the diagram above.

Next make a bight in the free end "B", and pull it up through the loop. Tighten by pulling the rope at A.

To prevent B slipping through the knot and losing the loop, tie a simple overhand knot near the end.

Sack knot

This knot holds the top of bags and sacks firmly closed and is good for fastening rubbish bags.

  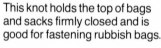 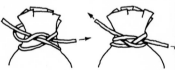

Hold the top of the bag together and place the string round it like this.

Then wind the string round and under the first cross-over, so that you make a figure of eight.

Finally, weave it round the front again, going over then under the string there.

Pull the free ends of the string to tighten the knot and close the bag securely.

Carrick bend

This is an excellent knot for tying two ropes together as it is very strong and will not slip, but can be easily untied if required.

Make a loop like this at one end of one piece of rope.

Lay the second rope right across the loop.

Then weave the end of it under and over the loop as shown.

Cross the rope back over itself and out under the loop. Pull tight.

Square lashing

This is used to join two sticks or poles together at right angles to each other. You will find it very useful for making camp gadgets.

Using one end of a length of cord, tie a clove hitch round the upright pole as shown.

Twist the short end of the cord round the long one, so it does not hang loose.

Take the cord up over the cross pole and round the back of the upright pole.

Then take it down over the left side of the cross pole and behind the upright pole again. Pull tight.

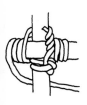

Repeat this three more times, pulling the cord as tight as possible after each round.

Take the cord back over the upright pole below the cross, and wind it round as shown.

Wind the cord round twice more, pulling very tightly to secure the lashing.

Finish off with a clove hitch round the cross pole.

Firewood

Wood from some trees burns better than that from others. If you are making a fire, whether for cooking or to keep yourself warm, it is wise to know which types of wood are best to use. Some types burn hotter or longer than others and some even burn when they are wet. So if you know a bit about different woods, you should be able to light a fire in any weather.

You need two types of fuel to light a fire successfully: kindling to start it and proper firewood for burning.

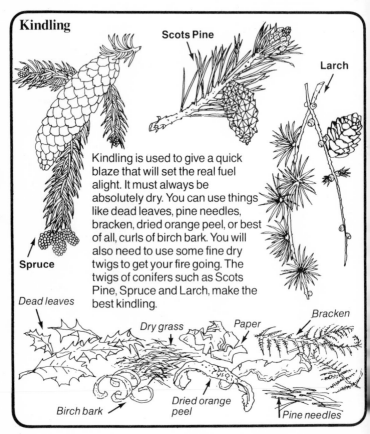

Kindling

Scots Pine

Larch

Kindling is used to give a quick blaze that will set the real fuel alight. It must always be absolutely dry. You can use things like dead leaves, pine needles, bracken, dried orange peel, or best of all, curls of birch bark. You will also need to use some fine dry twigs to get your fire going. The twigs of conifers such as Scots Pine, Spruce and Larch, make the best kindling.

Spruce

Dead leaves

Dry grass

Paper

Bracken

Birch bark

Dried orange peel

Pine needles

The best type of firewood comes from the hardwoods or broadleaved trees. Many hardwoods burn steadily and make a long lasting, warm fire which is also good for cooking. Try to find wood from the trees illustrated below if you can.

Always use wood that is dry rather than living, green wood or damp wood, and never burn any that is rotten, as it only smoulders and gives no heat. If you must use wood from the ground, first peel off the bark so that you remove the dampest part.

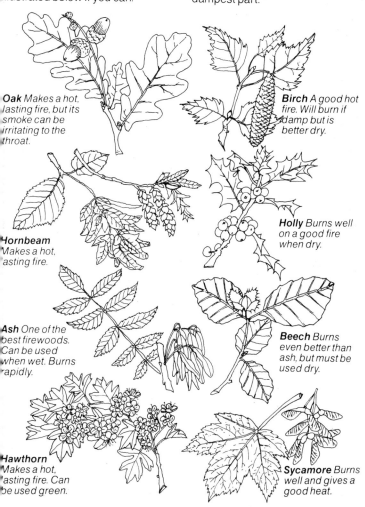

Oak *Makes a hot, lasting fire, but its smoke can be irritating to the throat.*

Birch *A good hot fire. Will burn if damp but is better dry.*

Hornbeam *Makes a hot, lasting fire.*

Holly *Burns well on a good fire when dry.*

Ash *One of the best firewoods. Can be used when wet. Burns rapidly.*

Beech *Burns even better than ash, but must be used dry.*

Hawthorn *Makes a hot, lasting fire. Can be used green.*

Sycamore *Burns well and gives a good heat.*

Wood to avoid

Some types of wood should be avoided when making a fire. They give off very little heat when burnt, and tend to smoulder and produce a bitter smoke. Do not use wood from the trees shown below.

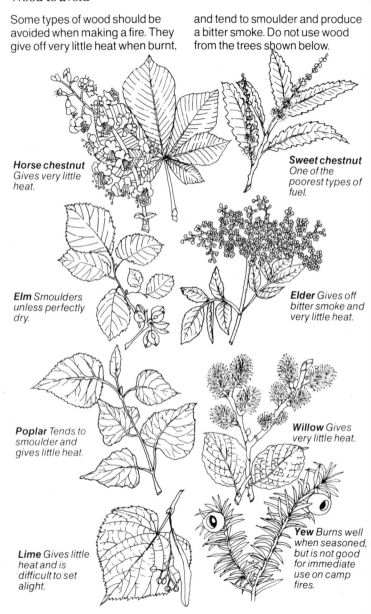

Horse chestnut *Gives very little heat.*

Sweet chestnut *One of the poorest types of fuel.*

Elm *Smoulders unless perfectly dry.*

Elder *Gives off bitter smoke and very little heat.*

Poplar *Tends to smoulder and gives little heat.*

Willow *Gives very little heat.*

Lime *Gives little heat and is difficult to set alight.*

Yew *Burns well when seasoned, but is not good for immediate use on camp fires.*

FIRST AID & EMERGENCIES

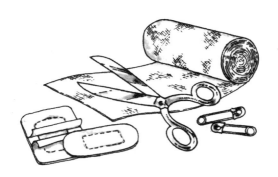

About First Aid

Outdoor activities such as walking and camping are fun, but one day you, or one of your friends, may have an accident. Accidents always happen unexpectedly, so it is vital that you know what to do immediately.

Pages 132 to 163 of this book tell you what to do in a serious emergency and how to treat general injuries and ailments. Practise some of the bandaging in your spare time and learn how to put someone into the recovery position.

Pages 164 to 187 show you how to deal with dangerous situations that might occur on land and water, and tell you about poisonous and dangerous plants and animals.

Assembling an emergency kit

Whenever you go walking, cycling or boating, take an emergency kit with you. Although you probably won't need it, you should always carry it with you just in case. Check the kit before you go out, and replace any items as they are used. Keep it simple; if it is too bulky it will be too heavy to carry very far. Most of the things needed can be bought cheaply or found around the house. Keep them in plastic bags or in a seal-top plastic box.

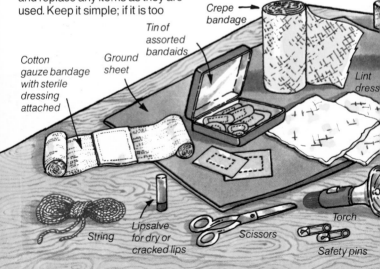

Crepe bandage

Tin of assorted bandaids

Cotton gauze bandage with sterile dressing attached

Ground sheet

Lint dress

String

Lipsalve for dry or cracked lips

Scissors

Torch

Safety pins

What is first aid?

First Aid is acting fast and doing all you can to help an injured person before professional help arrives. In a serious accident, your actions could even mean the difference between life and death. Even minor injuries should be treated carefully; if they are not attended to promptly they may become worse.

In any accident there are four things you must do before you attend to anything else:
1. Make sure that you are not in any danger yourself; it is much better to go and get help rather than put yourself in a situation where your own life may be at risk.
2. Check that the person is breathing; make sure that the airways are clear (page 139).
3. Stop any serious bleeding (pages 144/5).
4. Check that the person is conscious (pages 138/9).
ONLY when you have checked these things should you begin to worry about any other injuries. The order is easy to remember:
ABC

A = Airways
B = Bleeding
C = Consciousness

There is one other important thing to remember – the injured person will be upset and frightened. Reassure him and don't leave him alone. If help is needed, send someone else to organize it.

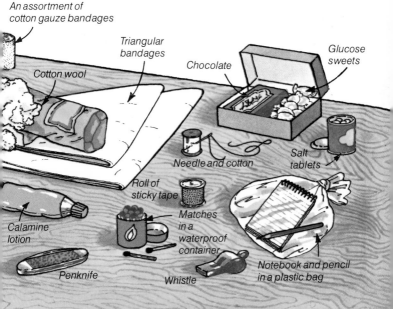

An assortment of
cotton gauze bandages

Triangular
bandages

Chocolate

Glucose
sweets

Cotton wool

Needle and cotton

Salt
tablets

Roll of
sticky tape

Calamine
lotion

Matches
in a
waterproof
container

Penknife

Whistle

Notebook and pencil
in a plastic bag

Getting help

Apply ABC emergency first aid *before* you go for help (page 133). *Never* leave an unconscious person alone. If someone is in need of urgent medical help – i.e. he is in danger of death, has severe injuries, or is in bad pain, send someone to find a telephone to call the emergency services. If he has minor injuries, call the local doctor. (If the number is not in the telephone directory, ask the operator.) In bad weather, don't let anyone go for help alone; wait until conditions improve.

If there is no-one else with you and the accident is really so serious that you must leave the person to get help, make sure that he is still breathing and conscious, and that bleeding has not started again. Make the person warm and as comfortable as possible, and tell him how long you think you will be away. If you think you will be away for some time, leave a whistle so that he can signal for help. Make sure you can find your way back to the place where you left the person.

Making an emergency call

The emergency number will be displayed in the phone box (999 in Britain). The call is free. The operator will ask you for your exchange, phone number and the service you want (fire, police or ambulance).

Fire

Describe where the fire is. Give brief details of the type of fire – car, house or forest – and whether anyone is trapped.

Police

If you are worried about what service to ask for, ring the police. They will contact the other services. Tell them your name and where you are.

Ambulance

Describe clearly where you want them to go, explain what has happened, how many people are hurt and the type of injuries.

Carrying a person with minor injuries

Human crutch

Pick-a-back

4-handed seat

If someone has a minor injury, help them to the nearest shelter or house. If the person is conscious and is capable of holding on to you, he could be carried by one of the methods shown here. Before moving anyone, check for serious injuries. If they are badly hurt don't move them in case you make the injury worse.

Road accidents

First make sure that you are not in any danger. Only move the casualty if he is in danger of being run over or the car is likely to explode. Get someone to warn approaching traffic and reduce any risk of fire by turning off the car engine; then attend to the casualty. Check that he is breathing (pages 136/7) and stop any heavy bleeding (pages 144/5). Deal with these three things first; minor injuries can be seen to later. Send for help and reassure the casualty. Listen to what he says about any pain, sickness or dizziness, which could indicate other injuries.

Breathing

To find out if someone is breathing, watch to see if his chest is rising and falling. If there are no signs of breathing, clear the mouth of any objects, blood, or vomit, so that the airways are clear. Tilt his head well back. If he does not begin to breathe, start artificial respiration.

Choking

Choking is caused by something blocking the airways. The person may or may not be coughing, but he will be red in the face. You must remove whatever is stuck in the throat before it stops him breathing. Thump him hard on the back several times to dislodge the object. Put a child head down over your knee, then thump him on the back. With a very young child, hold him up by the legs and slap him on the back. If, when you have removed the object, the person has stopped breathing (he will be white or blue in the face), start artificial respiration.

Suffocation

Suffocation is caused by something stopping air reaching the lungs. It may be an object (e.g. a plastic bag over the head) or smoke filling the airways. Remove anything over the face, or drag the person away from the danger. Start artificial respiration if breathing has stopped. If you are entering a smoke-filled room, first make sure you can get out. Go in on your hands and knees.

Artificial respiration

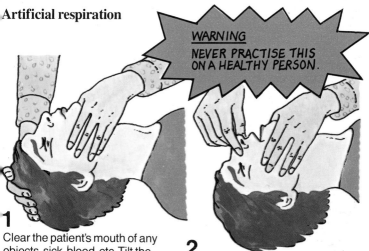

1
Clear the patient's mouth of any objects, sick, blood, etc. Tilt the head back with the chin pushed forward. This straightens out the airways and the person may start breathing again. If he does, put him in the recovery position (page 139).

2
If the person is breathing only faintly, or not at all, keep his head tilted back, open his mouth with one hand and with your other hand pinch his nostrils firmly together.

3

Take a deep breath. Cover his mouth with your lips and blow deeply into his lungs. Repeat this quickly four times so that you fill his lungs with air. Remove your mouth and wait for his chest to fall. If he fails to breathe, start artificial respiration again.

4
If he is still failing to breathe, there may be something stuck in his windpipe. Turn the person onto his side and thump him hard between the shoulder blades. Turn him back again. Put his head to one side and remove anything that is in his mouth. Tilt his head back with the chin forward and start artificial respiration again.

If breathing still fails to start, turn him on his side again and thump between the shoulder blades, then turn him back and remove anything in the mouth. Continue artificial respiration. Repeat these actions until breathing actually starts or help arrives.

Consciousness

If a person is unconscious don't waste time attending to small injuries; concentrate on making him breathe properly. There are different degrees of consciousness (explained below). Watch how the person is behaving so you can tell if his condition is getting any worse. Be prepared – people are often sick before they lapse into, or as they come round from unconsciousness.

The four stages of consciousness

a. Fully conscious: awake and able to talk.
b. Drowsy: keeps falling asleep, but is easily woken.
c. Stupor: only woken when pain is inflicted – try pinching the person. He will not be able to give proper answers to questions.
d. Cannot be woken at all. Pupils are dilated.

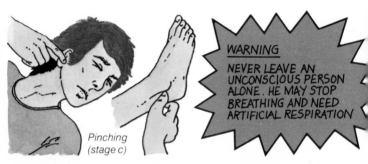

Pinching (stage c)

WARNING

NEVER LEAVE AN UNCONSCIOUS PERSON ALONE. HE MAY STOP BREATHING AND NEED ARTIFICIAL RESPIRATION

How to treat an unconscious person

Clear the mouth of any loose objects. With a hanky wrapped round your finger, wipe away any vomit, blood or loose teeth.

Loosen any tight clothing round the neck, waist and chest. Turn him over gently into the recovery position (see opposite).

The recovery position

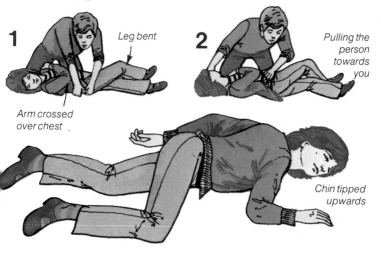

1 Leg bent

Arm crossed over chest

2 Pulling the person towards you

Chin tipped upwards

This is the best position for an unconscious person to lie in; the airways are clear so the person can breathe easily and will not choke. To put him in the recovery position, place the arm nearest you palm down underneath the body. Cross the other arm over the chest and bend the leg furthest

from you over the other one (1). Support the head with your hand and roll the person over by pulling on the clothes around the hips (2). Keep the airways open by tipping the chin upwards to straighten the neck. There is now little danger of the person choking; even so, don't leave him on his own.

Make him comfortable. If possible put a coat underneath him and cover him with another. Don't put anything under his head. He needs lots of fresh air, so keep back any crowds that may gather.

Keep a close check on his breathing. If it stops, start artificial respiration at once (pages 136/7). If he starts to come round, reassure him by talking. Be prepared for him to be sick.

Shock

Some degree of shock occurs after most accidents. Watch the injured person for signs of shock, even if the injury is minor. The worse the injury, the worse the shock. A serious state of shock can be very dangerous.

Signs to look for

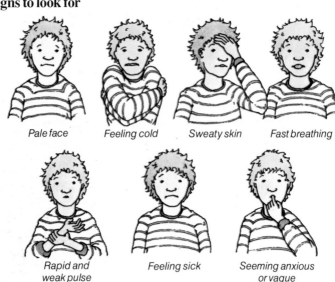

Pale face   Feeling cold   Sweaty skin   Fast breathing

Rapid and weak pulse   Feeling sick   Seeming anxious or vague

How to take someone's pulse

Blood is moved around the body by a pumping action of the heart. At certain points of the body you can feel a pulse which tells you how regular the pumping action is. A rapid and weak pulse is a sign of shock; an irregular pulse signals a possible heart attack.

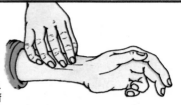

The easiest place to feel a pulse is on the wrist. Place your fingers just below the thumb joint on the wrist of your other hand. Move your fingers around until you find the pulse, then count the number of beats in 30 seconds. Multiply the number by two: this gives the

DON'T GIVE PATIENT A HOT WATER BOTTLE. THIS DRAWS BLOOD FROM HEART AND LUNGS TO THE SKIN. DO KEEP HIM WARM

DON'T GIVE DRINKS

LIE PATIENT DOWN WITH LEGS RAISED. (UNLESS THEY ARE BROKEN)

LOOSEN CLOTHING AT NECK, CHEST AND WAIST TO MAKE PATIENT COMFY

DON'T MOVE PERSON UNNECESSARILY, ESPECIALLY IF INJURIES ARE BAD

RAISE SHOULDERS AND TURN HEAD TO ONE SIDE IF HEAD, CHEST OR ABDOMEN IS INJURED

IF PATIENT IS SICK OR UNCONSCIOUS, PLACE IN RECOVERY POSITION

COVER WITH SHEET OR BLANKET TO PROTECT FROM COLD

IF PATIENT IS THIRSTY, WET LIPS WITH WATER

REMEMBER

DON'T HESITATE TO CALL AN AMBULANCE IF THE SHOCK OR INJURY IS SERIOUS

rate per minute.

Take your pulse again after some exercise and it will almost certainly be higher. The average adult pulse rate when resting is 60-80 beats per minute. The rate is higher in children: between 90 and 100 beats a minute. The rate varies from person to person. The main reason for taking a pulse is to see that it is regular and strong. The neck pulse can sometimes be easier to find, so try taking the pulse at the neck, as shown here.

Burns

Burns can be caused by contact with fire, hot objects, electricity, hot fat, boiling water, steam or dangerous chemicals. A burn causes loss of the liquid part of the blood, called plasma, from the tissues. The plasma either collects under the skin, forming blisters, or it leaks away if the skin is broken. The amount of plasma lost over a large area can be very serious. Never apply ointment. Only very minor burns should be bandaged. Concentrate on taking the heat out of the burn and then send for help. Treat for shock (pages 140/1).

Cool the burnt area

Apply cold water immediately to the burnt area. The faster you act, the less damage will be done. Use slow running water – a tap, hose or a running stream. If no running water is available, use a bucket of water but, if possible, avoid stagnant pond water. Leave the burn submerged for at least ten minutes. Running water should also remove any chemicals still sticking to the flesh.

If electricity has been involved, first make sure that the current has been switched off and is not still passing through the person's body (page 156); if he has stopped breathing, start artificial respiration (page 137).

Removing clothing

Don't remove charred clothing unless it is smouldering; it will have been sterilized by the burning. **Never remove any clothing stuck to a burn.** Though water should wash away any chemicals, do remove clothes that have been soaked by a chemical; be careful not to get chemicals on your hands.

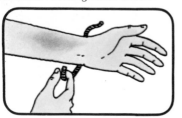

Take off anything tight, such as a watch or a shoe, before the area begins to swell.

Minor burns

First cool the injury for at least ten minutes under slow running water. Then, if the skin is unbroken, the affected area appears to be small, and, after half an hour, there is no blistering, treat it as a minor burn. If the area is still wet, gently dry it with cotton wool. Apply a sterile dressing and gently bandage (page 148).

Major burns

Wet cloth

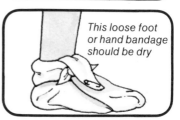

This loose foot or hand bandage should be dry

If the area has blistered or the skin is broken and weeping, this is a serious burn. Send for an ambulance. If possible, put the blistered area under slow running water and then cover with a cloth. If the burn covers a large area, you may not be able to place it under running water and it might be unwise to move the patient. In this case, gently cover the area with a wet cloth; keep wetting the cloth with cold water as it warms up. Get the person to lie down. If the burn is on a foot or hand you can gently tie a dry cloth into a bandage after the area has been cooled (Page 151 and above).

If the burn is on a limb, raise the limb and support it in a comfortable position to stop swelling. The person will probably be suffering from shock (pages 140/1), so loosen clothing round the neck, chest and waist and keep the person warm. If he is conscious, give him regular sips of cold water to replace the loss of plasma "water" from the wound. Give reassurance and watch for signs of severe shock.

Bleeding

Serious bleeding must be stopped immediately by applying pressure to the cut or wound with a roller bandage, a pressure pad, or the fingers. Don't apply a torniquet – it may cut off the blood supply completely and result in permanent damage. Send or go for help after you have applied first aid. The person may have lost a lot of blood, and this must be replaced by a blood transfusion in hospital.

What to do

If the wound is a clean cut, you can apply pressure by holding the cut edges together. If the bleeding is from a large area, use a dressing as a pressure pad, pressing it firmly over the area.

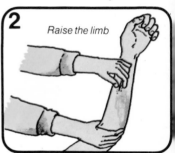

Dressing pad

If you have been holding the cut, apply a dressing (use material if no dressings are available). If there is glass or metal in the wound, put a ring pad over the dressing (page 147), then bandage.

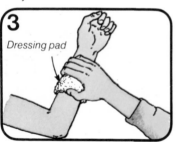

Raise the limb

If the injury is on a limb and there are no broken bones, hold the limb up so the blood flows away from the wound. Continue to apply pressure for at least ten minutes, even on a finger cut.

Gauze bandage

If bleeding is very bad, place another dressing over the first one to give more pressure. Bandage firmly with a roller bandage in the figure of eight manner (pages 148/9).

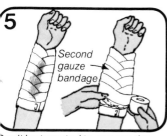

5

Don't be tempted to remove the bandage to look at the wound. You might restart the bleeding. If blood seeps through, add more pads and another bandage over the first one.

6

If the person appears to be suffering from shock (pages 140/1), get her to lie down and keep her warm. Raise her legs and rest them on a stone or rucksack so more blood goes to the head.

7

If much blood has been lost, the person will lose consciousness; put them into the recovery position (page 139). Send for help but don't leave the unconscious person alone.

Internal bleeding

Each person has, on average, about 6 litres (10 pints) of blood in his body. This circulates around the body in tubes or blood vessels called veins, arteries and capillaries.

A severe blow to the body may break blood vessels under the skin so blood leaks inside the body. Bruising is in fact bleeding under the skin.

Internal bleeding may not show on the skin as bruising if the injury is inside the body. If, after an accident, a person looks pale and ill, their skin feels cold (especially the hands and feet), and the pulse rate rises, they may be suffering from bad internal bleeding.

Other signs are a large swelling, very bad pain and/or severe shock. A lot of blood can be lost internally around broken bones: as much as two pints can be lost around a broken thigh bone.

The only first aid you can give to someone with internal bleeding is to raise the swollen limb *(unless it is broken)* and make the person rest. Treat them for shock (pages 140/1) and send or go for help.

Bandages

Bandages are used to hold a dressing in place, to put pressure on a wound so as to stop bleeding, or to hold still an injured part of the body. If possible, a wound should be covered with a clean dressing before it is bandaged. The most common types of bandages are roller and triangular. If, in an emergency, you haven't got your first aid kit, you can make dressings or bandages out of scarves, clothes or hankies.

Roller bandages

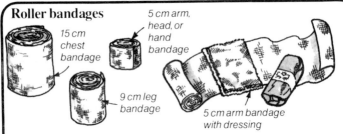

15 cm chest bandage

5 cm arm, head, or hand bandage

9 cm leg bandage

5 cm arm bandage with dressing

Roller bandages are made of elasticated crepe or cotton gauze. Crepe bandages are used when support is needed, for example when bandaging an injured joint. Cotton gauze roller bandages come in rolls of various widths for the different parts of the body; for example, finger bandages are 2.5 cm wide, leg bandages 9 cm wide, and chest bandages are 15 cm wide. You can buy gauze bandages with sterile dressings included in the packet. These bandages are also useful for putting pressure on badly bleeding cuts.

Triangular bandages

A triangular bandage is made of calico or linen, but in an emergency you can make one by cutting a one-metre square of material diagonally into two. This very useful all-purpose bandage can be made into a

Triangular calico bandage

sling or ring pad, or folded to make a narrow bandage which can be then used like a roller bandage (see opposite).

How to make a narrow bandage

Fold the point of the triangle over so it touches the base, then fold the bandage in half. This gives you a broad bandage, which could be used to hold a large dressing in place. The broad bandage folded in half makes a narrow bandage, which can be used to hold a dressing in place or to immobilize a limb (page 153).

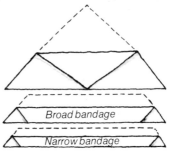

Broad bandage

Narrow bandage

How to make a ring pad

A wound over a possible fracture, or a wound containing grit or large splinters should be covered with a loose dressing. A ring pad placed on top will keep pressure off the wound when the bandage is applied.

With the end of a narrow bandage make a double loop around your hand. Take the loop off your hand and wind the bandage round it. Continue winding until you have made a firm ring. Tuck in the end. The ring pad should be large enough to encircle the wound.

Fastening bandages

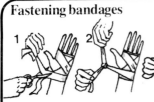

Wrap one end around the hand

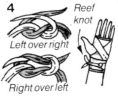

Reef knot

Left over right

Right over left

Bandages can be fastened with sticky tape or safety pins, or they can be tie-fastened. When using a safety pin, double the bandage end over to make a neat edge and then pin.

When tying a knot, cut the end of the bandage lengthwise into two (1). Knot these two ends to stop the bandage splitting (2). Then wrap one of the ends round the hand (3) and tie it to the other end (4). A reef knot is flat and tidy; it is easy to untie but it will not slip undone.

Using a roller bandage

Figure-of-eight roller bandaging is used to support an injured limb or joint. You also use this type of bandaging to hold a dressing in place over a cut.

Before bandaging, wash your hands. Cover an open wound with a dressing, being careful not to touch the wound or the underside of the dressing. If, however, the person is bleeding badly, don't worry about hygiene or correct bandaging – quickly wind a bandage firmly around the wound (see also pages 144/5)

Figure-of-eight roller bandaging

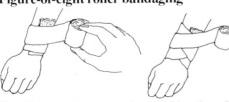

Face the person. Start by placing the bandage at an angle below the injury and on the dressing. Wind it firmly round twice to fix the dressing in place. Hold up the roll of bandage and, unrolling it a little at a time, start to wind it round the limb in a figure of eight. At each turn, overlap the previous wind of the bandage. Keep the bandaging at an even pressure. Finish above the injury with two firm turns on top of one another, then fasten.

Finger (cut, minor burn)

Fix the dressing in place with a couple of turns of the bandage (1). Criss-cross up the finger, away from the nail. Loop the bandage over the finger tip as shown (2). Criss-cross down the finger (3) and then back up again, so that you cover the loop. Finish at the base of the finger (4) and tie with a reef knot (page 147).

Elbow or knee (cut)

 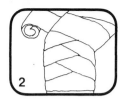 

If possible, use an elasticated crepe bandage for an elbow or knee; it gives support while allowing some movement of the joint. Hold the dressing in place with a couple of turns of the bandage; then criss-cross around the joint. Finish above the injury. Fasten a crepe bandage with a safety pin.

Hand or wrist (cut)

Hand

Wrist

For a hand wound, secure the dressing with a couple of turns of the bandage (1), then criss-cross up the hand (2). Take the bandage around the wrist to secure it; finish it here (3). For a wrist wound (4), criss-cross around the wrist, then secure the bandage with a couple of loops around the hand. Finish with a couple of turns around the wrist.

Foot or ankle (cut)

 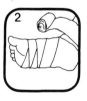 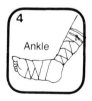

Foot

Ankle

For a foot wound, secure the dressing with a couple of turns (1), then criss-cross up the foot. Take the bandage around the ankle to secure it (2); finish here (3). For an ankle wound (4) criss-cross around the ankle then secure the bandage with a couple of loops around the foot. Finish with a couple of turns around the ankle. If the shoe has to be kept on, just bandage around the ankle.

Using a triangular bandage

Ordinary sling

Use this type of sling to give support to an injured arm. The arm may also need to be supported if the ribs have been injured. Hold the forearm of the injured side steady while applying the bandage. Lay the bandage

over the body as shown; the hand should be slightly higher than the elbow. Raise the lower point of the bandage and tie it to the point on the shoulder. The sling should now take the weight of the arm. Fold the point at the elbow and pin it.

Make-do slings

Pin sleeve to jacket

Padding

Padding

Turn up lower edge of jacket and pin to collar

Use a belt, scarf, or tie

Padding

Sling (badly injured arm, shoulder or collar bone)

Lay the arm across the chest, with the palm down. The hand should be higher than the elbow; this is a comfortable position and may reduce any swelling. Lay the bandage over the arm as shown. Hold the arm steady and ease the base of the bandage under the

hand, arm and elbow. Pass the lower end under the elbow and round the back to the uninjured shoulder. Tie the two ends in the hollow above the collar bone. Tuck the point in the crook of the elbow. Fold over the remaining material and pin.

Foot or hand (burn)

Put the foot (or hand) on the bandage and bring the point over the foot (or palm). Cross the two ends over the point and bring them around the back of the ankle (or wrist), then round to the front. Tie in front of the ankle (or on top of the wrist).

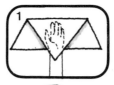

Turn point over knot and pin

1 Elbow or knee (burn)

Lay the bandage on the knee (or under the elbow). Bring the two ends around behind the knee (over the elbow), cross them over, bring them round to the front and tie. (For an elbow, tie behind the arm.)

1 Scalp (cut)

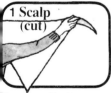 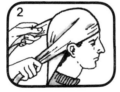 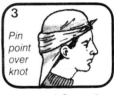

Pin point over knot

Turn over the long edge of the bandage to make a hem. Place this edge just above the eyebrows. Bring the ends down behind the head, keeping the ears uncovered. Cross the ends and tie in the middle of the forehead. Pin up the point.

Is the bandage too tight?

Bandages, especially roller bandages, must be applied firmly, but if they are too tight they can cut off blood circulation. Try taking the pulse. If you can't feel it, test to see if the bandage is too tight by pressing a finger-nail or toe-nail of the bandaged limb so that it turns white. The nail should turn pink again when the pressure is removed. If it stays white or blue, or if the fingers or toes are cold, numb or tingling, loosen the bandage slightly, but do not take it off.

Fractures and sprains

A fracture is a broken or a cracked bone. Without an X-ray it is difficult to tell a fracture from a sprain. Also, a sprain could have an underlying fracture, so treat a sprain as a fracture. Don't move someone with a fracture; you could cause more damage, especially if it is a complicated fracture; send for help.

Types of fracture

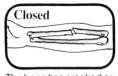 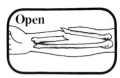 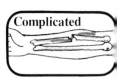

The bone has cracked or broken but is not sticking through the skin.

The broken bone is sticking through the skin making an open wound.

The broken bone has pierced a lung, nerve, blood vessels or the guts.

Sprains and dislocations

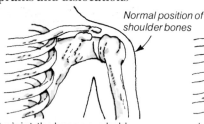 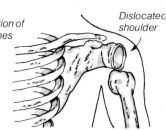

Normal position of shoulder bones

Dislocated shoulder

At a joint, the bones are held together by ligaments. An awkward fall or twist will tear or wrench these ligaments causing a sprain. A wrench may even push a bone right out of place; this is called a dislocation.

Signs of damage

The person will be in pain and may not be able to move his limb. Compare the injured side with the uninjured side. There may be swelling; any discolouration means internal bleeding which could be serious. If a nerve has been damaged there will be numbness and tingling.

What to do

Check to see that the person is breathing (pages 136/7). Do not move the injured part even if there is a lot of swelling – you could do more damage. Allow the person to keep the limb in a position which he feels to be as comfortable as possible.

Clean dressing

If the fracture is open (the bone will be sticking through the skin) and the wound is bleeding badly, squeeze the edges of the wound together. Hold the edges together until bleeding has stopped. Cover the wound with a clean dressing as quickly as possible to prevent any infection getting into the fractured bone. Don't bandage the wound. Send for help. Reassure the person, and stay with him.

Watch for signs of shock (pages 140/1). Make the person comfortable but don't give anything to drink. If the injury is on the lower limb, don't remove footwear. Steady a fractured leg to prevent further injury by padding either side with rolled-up clothes.

Falls

If someone has a fall when you are out, give ABC emergency first aid (page 133) and treat for shock (page 141). Don't move him or give him any drinks. Never try to straighten an injured limb. Send someone for help (page 134).

A bang on the head could mean a fractured skull; paralysis or a tingling sensation could mean that a nerve is trapped or the spine is injured. Don't move the person. However, if the person is unconscious, you must put him in the recovery position and stay with him.

If the injuries are minor, and you really must move the person because help is not available, you can support an injured arm with a sling (page 150). Use a four-handed seat, or a pick-a-back (page 135) to carry someone with a minor foot injury.

General injuries and ailments

Black eye

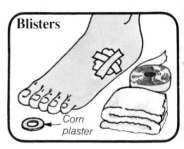

Blisters

The colour and swelling around a **black eye** is caused by bruising. Reduce the swelling by applying a cold compress or ice bag. Get the patient to a doctor; a blow that has resulted in a black eye may also have caused an eye injury or a skull fracture.

To make a cold compress, soak a cloth in cold water, squeeze out any excess water, and put it on the swelling. As the cloth warms up, soak it again in cold water.

To avoid getting **blisters,** wear well-fitting, comfortable shoes that have been "worn in". If your shoes do begin to rub, cover the sore area with a bandaid or a light, lint dressing held in place by sticking plaster. Ring-shaped corn plasters are useful for taking pressure off the blister. Don't burst the blister. If it has already burst, cut off the flap of skin and, if possible, let it dry out and heal in the open air.

Cramp

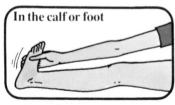

In the calf or foot

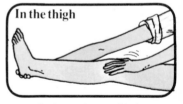

In the thigh

Cramp is caused by a muscle suddenly tightening up. To cure it, rub and stretch the cramping muscle. If it occurs in a calf or foot muscle, straighten the knee and pull the foot towards you. If the cramp is in the thigh, raise the leg with one hand under the heel and

press the knee down with the other hand. Someone who has been sweating a lot after hard exercise may get cramp. Give them one salt tablet or half a teaspoon of salt with a pint of water.

Dirty graze or minor cut (cleaning)

Roller bandage

Wash your hands before you put a dressing on a **cut**. Use lots of fresh water and some clean material to

bathe the cut. Start at the centre and wipe outwards. When the cut and the surrounding skin is free of dirt, dry

thoroughly and put on a bandaid or a clean dressing. If a cut is bleeding badly concentrate on stopping the bleeding.

Earache

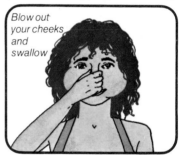

Blow out your cheeks and swallow

The best way to prevent **earache** in cold weather is to keep your ears warm by wearing a hat. If your ears ache after swimming, hold your nose and blow your cheeks

out while swallowing at the same time. If you have persistant earache you may have some sand or an infection in your ear. See a doctor at once.

Ear (an object in the ear) ▶

If you get something in your **ear** (or nose) don't try to get it out – you will end up pushing it further in. Go to a doctor who will remove it for you. If, however, an insect gets into the ear, it can be removed by *gently* flooding the ear with warm water or olive oil. The insect should float out. If you are stung inside the ear, see a doctor at once.

Bottle of olive oil

Electric shock

Don't touch anyone who may have been electrocuted; the electricity can pass through his body and severely injure you. Don't touch anything he is touching. Turn off the switch. Use an object, like a piece of wood, which is not wet, greasy, or made of metal, to push the person away from the source of power, or any wet surfaces. If you can't find a suitable object, pull him away by his clothing, being careful not to touch his flesh. If he has stopped breathing, give artificial respiration (page 137) then treat any burns (pages 142/3). Keep well away from anyone electrocuted by a pylon or a railway line. Go for help.

Eye (something in the eye) ▶

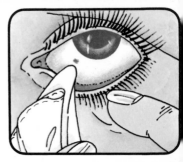

If something gets under the lower lid don't rub your **eye**; look up and pull the lower lid down. Using a damp, soft, clean cloth, gently lift the object out. If something is under the upper lid, look down and pull the upper lid over the lower one; this may dislodge the particle. If the object is on the pupil or is embedded in the eye, see a doctor.

Fainting

Put head between knees

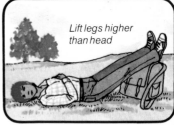

Lift legs higher than head

Fainting occurs when not enough blood reaches the brain; it results in temporary unconsciousness. The cause may be fright, bad news, lack of air or food. There may be some warning beforehand – feeling ill, giddy, or hot and sweaty. Tell the person to sit down; loosen any tight clothing around the neck. Put his head between his knees and tell him to breathe deeply. If, in spite of this, he faints, put his head to one side and lift his legs higher than his head. This will send more blood to the brain and he should recover in a matter of seconds. Slowly raise him into a sitting position. If he doesn't come round, put him in the recovery position (page 139).

Diabetes

If a diabetic, who has had his morning injection of insulin, becomes pale, sweaty and bad tempered and starts acting in an unreasonable manner, he is about to lose consciousness. Give him two tablespoons of sugar immediately. If he does lose consciousness, he is in danger of dying. Get help immediately.

Headaches

Rest and quiet are the best cures for a **headache**; a short nap or a cup of tea and a meal may also help. Headaches may be a symptom of something else such as stomach trouble. If the headache won't go away, see a doctor.

Hiccups

To get rid of **hiccups**, try holding the breath, breathing deeply or sipping warm water. A fright can sometimes stop hiccups.

Nosebleed ▶

Nosebleeds can be caused by a bad cold or a hit on the nose. Sit down with your head forward so that the blood does not run down your throat. Pinch the nostrils, just below the bony part of the nose, for about 15 minutes. Breathe through the mouth and do not blow your nose for a few hours. If the bleeding won't stop, see a doctor.

Fits

Many healthy people suffer from epileptic **fits.** Fits are not harmful, but they may come on without warning.

With a minor fit the person normally remains standing, but stares straight ahead and does not understand anything said to him. The fit should pass quite quickly. Afterwards, reassure the person, as he may not remember anything.

With a bad fit the person will fall down and become rigid. His arms and legs may jerk about, and he may become red in the face, or froth at the mouth. Don't try to hold him still, but do pull him away by his clothing if he is in a dangerous situation, or is likely to hit something and hurt himself. Be careful that he does not hit or kick you. Move any nearby furniture. When he has stopped jerking about, put a rolled-up hanky between his back teeth and lay him in the recovery position (page 139).

On coming round he will stay confused for some time. Keep an eye on him and, if possible, get him to rest.

Splinters ▶

If the **splinter** is just below the surface of the skin you may be able to remove it with a needle. Sterilize the needle by passing it through the hottest part of a flame. If the splinter is sticking out, try removing it with a pair of tweezers.

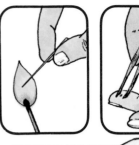

Sprays and pesticides ▶

Keep well away from any land which has been sprayed by low-flying aircraft or tractors.

Someone affected by **pesticides** may have a flushed face and shallow breathing. The poison can be absorbed through the skin, so remove the person from the area and take off any clothing covered with spray. Put him in a current of air and sponge his neck and back with cold water. Give

sweet drinks. If breathing stops, give artificial respiration (page 137). Take him to hospital as soon as possible.

Stitch

▲

A **"stitch"** is a sudden pain in the side. It usually occurs after exercise, especially if you are unfit. You may also get a "stitch" if you exercise too soon after eating a meal.

To relieve the pain, try bending over to touch your toes. If this doesn't work, rub the painful part and sip some water. Rest.

Tetanus

Tetanus or "lock jaw" is caused by a bacteria that gets into the body through cuts. If you get a cut when outside, from a garden tool, barbed wire, a rusty nail or an animal bite or scratch, go to a doctor for an anti-tetanus injection.

Toothache

You can ease **toothache** by putting a few drops of oil of cloves on your finger and rubbing the tooth. If the toothache occurs at the weekend when your dentist is closed, look in the phone book to see if there is a dental hospital nearby; they will usually see urgent cases.

Travel sickness

Before you start a long journey, take some pills recommended for **travel sickness**. Take paper bags with you in case of an emergency! When in a car, make sure there is plenty of fresh air, and ask for the car to be stopped if you feel sick. Do not read. Don't eat large meals before or during the journey. Sucking boiled sweets may stop you feeling sick, but don't eat chocolate.

Winding ▶

Winding is caused by a fall, or a blow in the solar plexus (the area just above the stomach). Winding can be very painful and makes breathing difficult. Put the person in the recovery position (page 139) and rub the area above the stomach. Loosen any tight clothing.

Vertigo (giddiness)

Vertigo is severe giddiness caused by fear of heights. If you find yourself with someone who is suffering from vertigo, encourage him to move on. Tell him to breathe deeply and get him to look up or ahead.

If you are on a path near a steep drop, guide the person away from the precipice, and walk between them and the edge.

Making a stretcher

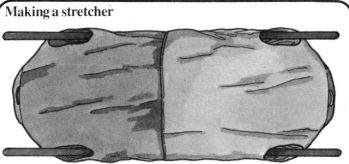

To make a stretcher, turn two coats or jackets the wrong way round, so the sleeves are inside. Button them up and pass two strong poles (tent poles would be ideal) through the sleeves of the coats. Test a home-made stretcher before you carry someone on it.

Never move someone who is seriously injured – you could do more damage.

Signalling for help

Shouting is not the best way to get help, but if someone is injured and you think that there is help nearby, cup your hands round your mouth, and shout something like "Cooee". This sound will travel further than a short cry like "help". Make signals with objects that can be left on show, or signals that can be repeated

at regular intervals; they should have a specific meaning. Don't waste torch batteries or fuel – you may need them later.

Shadow writing

SOS is the best known distress message. Mark SOS out on the ground by piling earth, stones, leaves and clothing into the shape of the letters. The sun or the moon shining on the letters will cast shadows which will outline them. Make each letter as big as possible, about 7-10 metres long, so they will attract a pilot's attention.

Smoke signals

On clear days, attract attention with white smoke. Burn anything damp, like moss, clothes, green branches or leaves.

On dull days, make black smoke by burning rubber, grease or oil; but if fuel is scarce, save it until rescue is in sight.

Three of anything is known internationally as a distress signal. Light three fires in a triangle about 100 paces apart.

Kites and flags

Lay a handkerchief, or a square of material torn from a piece of clothing, on the ground. Try and use a colour that will stand out from the background.

Tie two sticks together in the form of a cross and lay them on the handkerchief. Tie the ends of the sticks to the corners of the handkerchief with some string.

Make a tail with a piece of bandage. Tie a ball of string to the kite at the three points on the sticks as shown.

Write SOS on the cloth, and fly the kite.

If there is no wind, make a flag to wave by attaching a square of cloth to a stick.

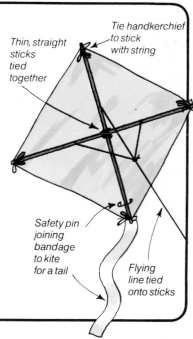

Tie handkerchief to stick with string

Thin, straight sticks tied together

Safety pin joining bandage to kite for a tail

Flying line tied onto sticks

Ground-to-air signals

Directed signals

Use these signals when possible rescue is in sight. Save your torch batteries and fuel for these moments. You can signal directly at the aeroplane or rescue team with a torch or any sort of shiny object: a mirror, a knife blade, a piece of shiny metal, or a tin lid.

Tin lid

When it is sunny, aim a signal by using a tin lid that is shiny on both sides and has a small hole punched in the middle. Hold it 15 centimetres from your face and look through the hole at the target. Sunlight will form a spot of light on your face which will be reflected on the lid. While looking at the target through the hole, alter the angle of the lid until the light spot disappears. Your target will now receive the flash.

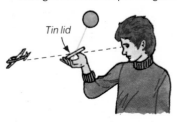

Tin lid

If the angle between the target and sun is very large, hold the tin lid so a spot of light falls on your hand. Look at the target through the hole and adjust the lid until the reflection of the light spot on your palm disappears.

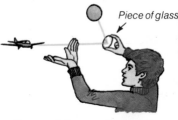

Piece of glass

If you only have a piece of glass, raise the glass in one hand and blot out the target with the other. Reflect the sunlight until it hits your hand. When you lower your hand you will be signalling directly at the aeroplane.

Standard body signals

There are signals that you can use when the rescuer can actually see you. They are all internationally-known signals, recognized by airmen all over the world. By using them you can "speak" to your rescuers. Use your body as a sign, or mark the signs out with stones, clothing or whatever materials are available.

Yes   No

● Don't give up.
● Be prepared for rescue.
● Encourage people with you.
● Keep signalling.

Medical assistance needed urgently

Don't land here   *Land here*

International ground-to-air signals

Doctor needed

First Aid needed

Unable to go any further

Food and water needed

Yes

No

REMEMBER
WHEN YOU HAVE BEEN RESCUED, CLEAR AWAY YOUR SIGNALS, OTHERWISE SOMEONE MAY WASTE TIME TRYING TO RESCUE YOU AGAIN!!

Heat hazards

In hot and humid climates, the body tries to cool itself by sweating. This results in salt and water loss. Too great a loss of water and salt will result in heatstroke and heat exhaustion. If this occurs, drink a pint of water with half a teaspoon of salt dissolved in it, or take a salt tablet with the water.

Heatstroke

The signs are a high temperature, hot, dry skin and possibly delirium and collapse. Send for help. While you are waiting, get the person's temperature down by fanning him. Wrap him in a wet shirt and put a damp cloth on his face and neck.

Heat exhaustion

The signs are a headache, cramp, feeling sick, clammy and dizzy. Get the person to rest in the shade and give him salt and water.

Sunburn

The sun can actually burn your skin; a minor burn will be red and itchy, a more serious burn will cause blistering. Water reflects the sun's rays that cause sunburn, so be particularly careful near the sea. Keep your head, neck and shoulders covered, especially at midday when the sun is at its hottest. If you do get burnt, rest in the shade and drink some water. Apply calamine lotion to the red areas. If you have bad blistering, see a doctor.

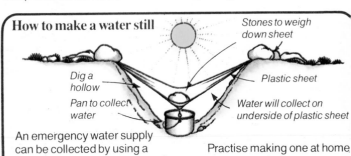

How to make a water still

Stones to weigh down sheet

Dig a hollow

Plastic sheet

Pan to collect water

Water will collect on underside of plastic sheet

An emergency water supply can be collected by using a home-made water still.

Practise making one at home on a sunny day.

Sun and snow blindness

Soot or dirt

Card with slits

Band of grass or leaves

Two handkerchiefs knotted together

Handkerchief over face and ears

Hair

Sunglasses

Newspaper hat

The reflection of the sun's rays from snow and water can damage your eyes as well as burn your skin. The pictures above show some of the ways that you can protect your eyes. If you do get sore eyes, cover them with cold compresses (see page 154). As the compresses warm up, wet them again with cold water.

DO'S...

DO SIT IN THE SHADE

DO BOIL WATER FROM PONDS AND STREAMS BEFORE DRINKING IT

DO WEAR LIGHT-COLOURED CLOTHES — THEY REFLECT HEAT

DO KEEP CLOTHES ON — THIS STOPS SWEAT EVAPORATING TOO FAST

DO WIPE FACE, BROW AND BACK OF NECK WITH WATER TO KEEP COOL

DO EAT LITTLE AND OFTEN

... & DON'TS

DON'T WALK IN THE HOTTEST PART OF THE DAY

DON'T DRINK SEA WATER

DON'T WEAR DARK CLOTHES — THEY ABSORB HEAT

DON'T EAT LARGE MEALS — DIGESTING USES A LOT OF WATER

Cold hazards

The effects of exposure to the cold can be very serious, so protect yourself by wearing a hat to keep your head warm, a scarf wrapped round your face, goggles if it is very cold, gloves and warm socks. Eat regularly to give yourself energy and stop and rest if you get tired.

Keeping warm

DO'S....   ..& DON'TS

DO KEEP MOVING AND JUMP ABOUT

DO BLOW ON FINGERS AND SLAP ARMS ACROSS CHEST

DO MAKE FACES

DON'T SIT ON COLD, WET GROUND. PUT DOWN LEAVES, BRANCHES OR A PLASTIC SHEET FIRST

DO WEAR ALL YOUR CLOTHES, PUT PAPER BAGS OVER HANDS AND FEET.

DO LIGHT A FIRE. A FEW SMALL FIRES WILL BE WARMER THAN ONE BIG ONE

DO EAT HOT FOOD AND DRINK

DON'T GET TOO HOT AND SWEATY — SWEAT CAN FREEZE

Frostbite

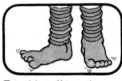
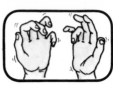

Frostbite affects the parts of the body that are most exposed, such as the fingers, toes, nose, ears and chin. Signs of frostbite are numbness and waxy-looking skin. If you haven't got gloves, put socks on your hands. Wiggle your feet, hands and face to keep the blood flowing. Warm a frost-bitten area slowly; don't try and thaw out in front of a fire.

Exposure

Exposure is caused by continuous chilling from wind, rain and cold. Signs are a general slowing down, blurred speech or eyesight, shivering fits and eventually collapse.

Stop at once and find or make a shelter (ways of sheltering are shown below).

Remove any wet clothes. Put on dry ones. Cover your head, neck and hands.

Get inside a sleeping bag or wrap yourself in a blanket. Cover it with a plastic sheet or spare clothes.

All huddle together. Two people may be able to get into one sleeping bag for extra warmth.

Drink something hot and eat energy-giving foods such as sugar, chocolate, glucose sweets, nuts and dates.

Shelters

Stretch a plastic sheet against a stone wall or boulder. Put something on the ground to sit on and get into your sleeping bag.

Put on extra clothes. Take your arms out of your jacket sleeves and warm them in your armpits. Put your feet in your rucksack.

Shelter behind a boulder. Hug your knees to keep warm.

Make a hollow beside a fallen tree. Use dead branches for a roof.

Make a circle of stones and rocks and huddle together.

Fires in forest and grassland

Fire can be terrifying when out of control. It can spread very fast, sometimes faster than you can run, especially if there is a strong wind. Notice in which direction the fire is spreading. Don't run blindly through the flames. Look for a path, or head for open ground. Cover your face and as much of your body as possible with clothes and blankets. Stay together and keep your face as near to the ground as possible, where the air is most fresh.

Fires at camp

If you can't get hold of water to put out a small fire, smother the flames by shovelling sand or soil over them. You can also beat out the flames with branches or coats.

Trapped in a car

If the fire is on either side of the road, stay in the car and tell the driver to drive fast until you are out of the danger area. Keep all the windows and air vents tightly closed. If the flames are completely surrounding the car, you must still try to drive out of danger. If the car is stationary, the metal body will heat up and the car will act like an oven.

1 Escaping from fire

Try and reach any nearby water and, if you can swim, leap in and wait until the fire has passed. Don't try to outrun the fire, as you will probably be overcome by the heat.

2

If there is no water nearby, scrape a small hollow behind a log or large boulder and lie face down as flat as possible. Cover as much of your body as you can with clothing, blankets or earth.

3

If you are in front of the fire, and you can see a wide path where there are few flames, cover as much of your body as possible, take a deep breath and run through the area as fast as you can.

Clothes on fire

If your clothes catch fire, wrap yourself in the nearest material to hand eg. a coat, blanket or ground-sheet. Leaving your head sticking out, roll over and over on the ground. If someone else is on fire, first pull them to the ground, then wrap them in the nearest available material. If you have wrapped them in something synthetic and it has melted, don't try to remove the material after the flames have been put out – you may pull away burnt skin (pages 142/3).

Natural disasters

Most types of weather conditions will be forecast in advance, so always listen to the local radio before going out. If you do get caught in bad weather, don't struggle on getting cold, wet and tired. Look for shelter.

Lightning

Lightning is attracted to metal such as wire fences, and to solitary boulders, single trees and water. Keep well away from anything standing on its own.

Seek shelter in a wood (avoid the tallest trees), or in the middle of a flat field. Either crouch on the ground, lie on your air mattress or cover yourself with a groundsheet. Make sure that you are not near anything metal, such as a rucksack frame. If someone is hit by lightning and survives, they will have very bad burns (see pages 142/3 and 140/1).

High winds

In strong winds, never walk on narrow mountain ledges or peaks: you could get blown off by a gust. If it suddenly becomes windy, tuck your clothes into your trousers; a flapping coat or jacket can catch the wind and throw you off balance. If the wind is very strong, lie flat on the ground.

Fog, rain and sleet

When you set out walking, you should always carry emergency rations, a waterproof and a spare jumper in case the weather turns bad and you have to stop and shelter. In hilly country, mist can appear very suddenly. You must stop and shelter. It is easy to get lost and you may walk over the edge of a rock face. Stay together.

Floods

Try to avoid camping close to a river. There is a possibility of heavy rain occurring up river and flood water could come rushing down when you are asleep or away from the tent. If there is a flood warning, take food, drinking water and spare clothes, and make for high ground. If you are swept away by flood water, try to grab hold of a floating object such as a log or a piece of wood. If it is big enough, climb on top and use it as a raft. Paddle to safety, using your hands or a piece of wood.

Quicksand and bog

Watch out for quicksands in river beds, especially tidal estuaries and sandy beaches, and for bogs or moors. Clumps of reeds and grasses growing far apart may be a sign of boggy ground.

Throw yourself flat; you will only sink deeper if you struggle. Take off your rucksack and try to put it underneath you. Roll and twist until your feet are free, then "swim" across the bog.

171

Blizzards

If you are caught in a heavy blizzard, try and find shelter where you can rest instead of struggling on getting cold and tired. If you can't see a hut or shed nearby, you can make a natural shelter from drifts around trees and boulders.

Tree shelter
- Plastic sheet
- Don't lean against the sides
- Boughs and snow on top
- Floor of boughs and bark

Scoop out a hole at the side of a tree or boulder and build up a rim around the hole with the snow you dig out. Spread a plastic sheet across it to make a roof; hold it down with snow. Cover the roof with branches or more snow to keep in warmth. Lay a plastic sheet, branches, or bark over the "floor" of the hole.

Earthquakes

If you are in a building when earthquake tremors start, don't run out into the street. Wait in a doorway where you can shelter from falling rubble. If you are in the street, crouch down in the middle of the road with your arms over your head.

Tornadoes

Tornadoes are whirling, funnel-shaped wind storms which suck up everything in their path. Lie flat on the ground, if possible in a cave or hole in the ground. In a building stay away from windows; try to get down to the cellar or basement.

Avalanches

Avalanches are extremely dangerous and can happen very suddenly; they are especially likely to occur during a thaw and after a new fall of snow. Listen to the weather forecasts for your area; if there are any warnings of avalanches don't go out walking or skiing.

Get rid of your skis, ski sticks, ice axes, etc. Try and grab hold of a tree or a rock and hang on. Keep your head down.

If you are swept down with the snow, "swim" with it, trying to keep your head above the surface. Keep your mouth shut.

As the avalanche stops, make a final effort to get to the surface. If you are buried, scoop a hole around your face before the snow freezes. Find out which way up you are by spitting; if the spit lands on your face, you are lying on your back.

REMEMBER
WHEN YOU ARE SKIING OR WALKING ALWAYS STICK TO SKI RUNS OR PATHS. GO IN A GROUP OF AT LEAST THREE.

Danger on water

Accidents can easily happen because people do not take proper care near water. Before you go near any open water, you must be able to swim. Learn in a pool where the shallow and deep ends are marked and there are no currents to swim against. If you are not a strong swimmer, don't go out of your depth.

Find out where it is safe to swim. Beaches with lifeguards fly a red and yellow flag when it is safe, a red one when it is not safe.

Don't swim around sluices, bridges, piers, wrecks or in strong tides, where there will be currents to swim against.

Never dive into water unless it is at least two metres deep, and you can see that the bottom is clear of any rocks or objects.

Don't clamber about on rocks with bare feet. Rocks, shells and sea urchins can cut your feet. Always wear non-slip shoes.

Never play with or lie on an air bed on open water unless it is tied to something on the shore. You could be swept out to sea.

Don't swim straight after a meal, or when you are hungry. Wait for two hours after you have eaten.

Don't stay too long swimming in the water. You can get cold and tired and are therefore more likely to get cramp (page 154).

In open water, swim along the shore rather than out to sea. If you go out too far you may find it difficult to get back.

Don't wade out to sandbanks or around rocky headlands, and don't explore caves. You may get cut off by the tide.

Don't mess around in the water, duck other people or pretend to drown. Don't take any "dares" like swimming out to distant points.

Boats

IF YOU CAPSIZE KICK OFF HEAVY BOOTS AND TAKE OFF ANY OUTER CLOTHING.

Before you take a boat out, find out about the local currents and the times of the tides. Only go out in fine weather, and tell someone where you are going. Don't go out alone. Always wear a life-jacket and take some warm, waterproof clothes and some food with you.

DON'TS

DON'T OVERLOAD A BOAT

DON'T STAND UP OR CHANGE PLACES

DON'T WEAR WELLINGTONS

DON'T GO NEAR OTHER BOATS, ROCKS OR WEIRS

Saving others from water

Only someone experienced in life-saving should swim out to rescue a drowning person. Drowning people panic, and may clutch at the rescuer causing both to drown. So act quickly, go and get help or use one of these methods of rescue.

Victim near bank

Lie flat and hold onto something secure on the bank. Grab the person's wrist (don't let them grab you), or hold out something for them to grab. Let go if you are being dragged into the water.

Victim further out

If the victim is quite far out, throw a rope or anything that floats – a life-belt, swimming ring, beach ball, plank of wood. Don't aim it directly at him; throw it within easy reach!

An object with a line attached is best so you can pull the victim ashore. Hold the line up as you pull him in, to lift him slightly out of the water.

Victim quite far out in shallow water

Make a human chain. The person nearest the shore holds onto something secure, while the others grasp wrists, facing in opposite directions, until someone can reach the victim or throw them a floating object. If you are alone, wade in and try to get near enough to get hold of the victim or to throw him something. Lean backwards and get a firm foothold before you grab hold of him.

Victim a long way out

ONLY ATTEMPT THIS IF YOU CAN ROW WELL

Stern

If, and *only* if, you know how to row well and can handle the type of boat available, row out to the rescue. Approach stern first with the bow facing head on to any current. This is important because the person could capsize you by grabbing the side of the boat. Tell him to hold on to the stern and, if you have a rope, put it under his armpits and tie him to the boat. Tow him ashore, making sure his face is clear of the water. Don't try to get him aboard because you may capsize the boat. If you haven't got a rope, wait with him until help arrives.

Lifebelt

ONLY ATTEMPT THIS IF YOU ARE A GOOD SWIMMER

If no boat is available, and if, and *only* if, you are a very good swimmer, you can swim out to the rescue with a floating object. Make sure first that you can manage the distance; take off bulky clothes and shoes. Although time is important, don't swim so fast that you get tired – remember that you've got to swim back again. Push the floating object towards the person so that he grabs the object rather than you; stay well clear of him. You can then wait until help arrives, return alone to get help, or swim back with him.

Saving yourself from water

Inflate your life jacket. Stay with the boat so you can use it to hang on to, and so you will be seen more easily by rescuers.

Hang on to the oars or paddles if you can, but don't risk losing the boat; it could get swept away by wind or currents.

Tie yourself to the boat, so that you won't lose it if you get tired and lose your grasp.

Signal by holding up an oar with a piece of brightly coloured clothing tied to it.

If there is a storm and it is difficult to hold on to the boat, swim underneath and hang on to the seats until the weather improves.

If you lose the boat and are getting tired, relax by floating. Keep your chin and face out of the water.

Save warmth and energy

REMEMBER
ALWAYS WEAR
YOUR LIFE
JACKET.

Keep on one layer of clothing to retain some heat. Save energy and stay warm by holding your arms tight against your sides with your knees raised. If there are several of you, keep your arms around each other.

How to make a lifebelt

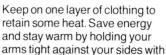

You can make a "lifebelt" with trousers, but a shirt is easier, since you lose less energy taking it off. Take your arms out of the sleeves; do up the top two buttons, and swivel the shirt round (1). Raise the bottom of the shirt (2). Bring the shirt down quickly so air is trapped under it (3). As the air leaks out, trap some more.

How to get into a lifebelt

This is not as easy as it looks, so practise a few times in the local baths. Push the side nearest to you underwater, so that the other side sticks up. Push the bottom edge away from you so that the belt begins to fall over your head. As it drops over your head, raise one arm and put it through, then put the other arm through.

Landing on rocks

If you have to land on rocks, aim for a point where the waves are calmest. Ride in on a wave with your feet forward to act as a buffer.

Lurch forward, try and get a hand-hold, then scramble on to the rocks as quickly as possible before you are pulled off by the se

If trapped by an incoming tide ...

Don't attempt to climb a cliff face if it has no footholds or is too high.

Don't climb a cliff face which look crumbly, or which might have loose rocks further up.

Look for a secure ledge above the high tide mark, and wait until the tide goes out again.

If your shoes are slippery, take them off; either climb in socks, or put socks over your shoes.

REMEMBER

IF YOU ARE GOING FOR A WALK ON THE BEACH, ALWAYS CHECK THE TIMES OF TIDES SO THAT YOU DON'T GET CUT OFF.

Points to remember

Whatever you are doing – walking, cycling or sailing, always go out in a group of at least three. If you are going rowing or sailing, always wear a life jacket.

Before you go out, check the weather forecast in the paper or on radio or television in case bad weather is on the way.

Work out a plan of your route; leave a copy with someone saying where you are going and what time you expect to be back.

Some camp sites have message boxes which are checked. Leave your route and expected return time there.

REMEMBER
REMOVE MESSAGES ON YOUR RETURN, OTHERWISE A SEARCH PARTY MIGHT BE SENT OUT TO LOOK FOR YOU

When out and about

DO GO OUT IN A PARTY OF AT LEAST THREE

DO TAKE MAP, COMPASS AND EXTRA CLOTHES

DO LOOK FOR SHELTER IF THE WEATHER BECOMES STORMY

DON'T WALK AFTER DARK. IF YOU HAVE TO, FACE ONCOMING TRAFFIC AND USE YOUR TORCH

NEVER HITCH-HIKE ALONE, EVEN IN EMERGENCIES

Poisonous plants

Never eat any berries, nuts, seeds, roots, leaves, or flowers on a plant unless you definitely know that they are edible. Don't think that the plant is edible just because an animal has been eating it; the animal may not be affected by the poisons. Avoid red berries – they are usually poisonous. Don't eat any mushrooms or toadstools in the wild – it is easy to confuse poisonous and edible ones.

Plants poisonous to the touch

Poison Ivy

Poison Sumac

Poison Oak

The plants shown above are all found in North America, and are poisonous to the touch. They will bring you out in a rash or blisters.

If you touch one, wash with soap and water. The poisons can be carried in smoke, so don't burn the wood of these plants.

Deadly poisonous plants

Red

Black

Holly
*Poisonous berries,
Symptoms: very bad
sickness.*

Red

Yew
*Poisonous leaves,
berries. Symptoms:
sickness, diarrhoea,
clammy skin, trembling.*

Deadly Nightshade
*Poisonous berries.
Symptoms: high
temperature, great thirst.*

Yellow

White

Purple

Laburnum
*All parts are poisonous.
Symptoms: burning in
mouth and throat,
headache, stomach-
ache.*

Hemlock
*All parts are poisonous.
Sore throat, muscular
weakness, trembling,
sickness.*

Foxglove
*All parts are poisonous.
Symptoms: stomach-
ache, headache,
sickness, dizziness,
drowsiness.*

Deadly poisonous fungi

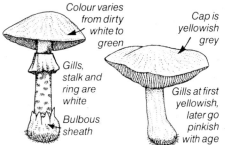

Colour varies from dirty white to green

Cap is yellowish grey

Gills, stalk and ring are white

Bulbous sheath

Gills at first yellowish, later go pinkish with age

Red cap with white warts

Gills, ring and stalk are white

Fly Agaric
Symptoms appear half an hour to four hours later: sickness, giddiness, visions.

Death Cap
Symptoms appear many hours later: sickness, great pain, diarrhoea, collapse, coma.

Livid Entoloma
Symptoms appear soon: sickness, weakness, diarrhoea, pain.

Food poisoning and its three main symptoms

You can get food poisoning from eating bad food. Avoid stale food, or food that smells "off". Canned food can also go off; if a can is badly dented or punctured, or bulges at one end, throw it away.

1

2

3

Pain and cramp around the stomach

Diarrhoea; feeling sick.

Possible headache; blurred vision, dizziness; weakness.

WHAT TO DO IF SOMEONE IS POISONED

1. PHONE FOR AN AMBULANCE.
2. IF NO HELP IS AT HAND, YOU COULD TRY TO MAKE YOURSELF SICK BY STICKING YOUR FINGERS DOWN YOUR THROAT.
3. PUT AN UNCONSCIOUS PERSON IN THE RECOVERY POSITION.
4. TAKE SOME OF THE BERRIES OR LEAVES THAT HAVE CAUSED THE POISONING TO THE HOSPITAL WITH YOU.

Animals that sting

Bees, hornets and wasps

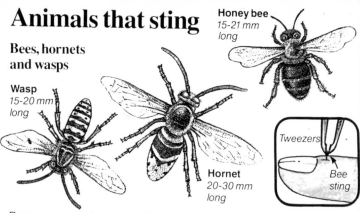

Honey bee
15-21 mm long

Wasp
15-20 mm long

Hornet
20-30 mm long

Tweezers

Bee sting

Bees, wasps and hornets will normally leave you alone as long as you leave them alone, so don't rush around trying to swat them: they may get angry and sting you. Keep calm and wait until they fly off. Bees sting only once and then die; wasps and hornets can sting more than once. Bees leave their sting in the flesh; get it out quickly with your fingernails, a pair of tweezers or a sterilized needle. Don't squeeze a sting – you will push the poison further into the flesh. Don't scratch it – this will make it itch more. The irritation usually wears off after an hour or so.

Stings in the mouth

Watch out for wasps and bees when eating sweet food. If someone is stung in the mouth or throat, call a doctor. While waiting for help get them to wash their mouth with a solution of bicarbonate of soda (one teaspoonful in a glass of water). If breathing is difficult, put them in the recovery position (page 139).

Bee swarms

If you find yourself next to a disturbed nest, stay still for a few minutes until the bees have calmed down, then move slowly away. About once a year bees look for a new nest site; they leave the old nest in a great swarm. Don't panic if a swarm comes near you; they are not attacking and will ignore you.

Removing ticks

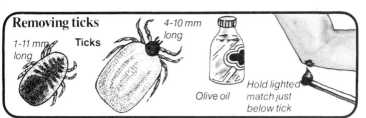

Ticks 1-11 mm long

4-10 mm long

Olive oil

Hold lighted match just below tick

Ticks feed on blood. They bury their mouthparts into the skin and cling on firmly while feeding. If you are camping, keep a watch for ticks on your skin, as they can pass on diseases. They are difficult to pull out as their body often breaks off leaving the head embedded. You can get them to drop off by holding a lighted match near them, but you may also burn yourself. The best way to remove a tick is to coat it with oil. Leave the oil on for a while and then pull the tick out with a pair of tweezers.

Mosquitoes

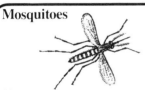

Mosquito bites give you itchy lumps; these will keep itching for several days and can be very irritating when you get hot. Mosquitoes are not dangerous, but in the tropics they can pass on malaria. Use an insect-repelling cream and keep as much of your skin covered as possible. Camp on high ground away from swampish water where mosquitoes breed. They are attracted to body heat and sweat, so even though you may be feeling hot, keep you clothes on at night to protect your skin.

Treating insect bites

Calamine lotion

Soap

Bicarbonate of soda

Don't scratch an insect bite. This will only make it itch more, and dirt under your finger nails may get into the bite and cause an infection. To keep the swelling down, apply a paste of bicarbonate of soda (use spit if you have no water); calamine lotion may reduce the itching. If you have nothing else, soap or even mud spread over the bite will help.

Dangerous animals

Snakes

Leave snakes alone – don't try to kill them. They will want to escape rather than attack, and will bite only in order to defend themselves.

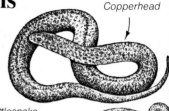

Copperhead

Rattlesnake

Adder

Taipan

Common Brown Snake

THIS WARNING APPLIES TO ANY POISONOUS BITE

GET THE PERSON TO HOSPITAL AS SOON AS POSSIBLE. TRY TO REMEMBER WHAT THE ANIMAL LOOKED LIKE SO THAT THE HOSPITAL WILL KNOW WHAT ANTI-VENOM TO GIVE. KEEP THE PERSON CALM. GET HIM TO LIE DOWN. WASH THE BITE WITH SOAP AND WATER IF POSSIBLE. SUPPORT AND IMMOBILIZE THE LIMB. GET MEDICAL HELP IMMEDIATELY. IF BREATHING STOPS, GIVE ARTIFICIAL RESPIRATION (SEE PAGE 9)

DO'S....

...& DON'TS

DO WEAR THICK SOCKS AND STRONG SHOES

DO WALK NOISILY. SNAKES ARE TIMID CREATURES AND DON'T WANT TO MEET YOU

DON'T PUT YOUR HANDS IN HOLES OR CREVICES. MAKE SURE YOU LOOK WHERE YOU PUT THEM

Jellyfish

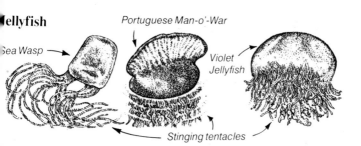

Portuguese Man-o'-War

Sea Wasp

Violet Jellyfish

Stinging tentacles

The jellyfish shown above can give you very nasty stings that can be fatal. Most jellyfish stings, however, are not dangerous; they can be treated by pouring methylated spirits or alcohol over the area. Calamine lotion will ease the pain. If you do come across small jellyfish when swimming, splash them out of the way.

Spiders and scorpions

Sydney Funnel Web Spider

Black Widow

Scorpion

Britain has no scorpions and no poisonous spiders. However, there are poisonous species in warmer parts of the world. Scorpions usually live in rocky areas and in stone walls. Spiders can be found under rocks, logs, in holes and crevices and sometimes in houses.

Rabies

Rabies is a dangerous disease that has no cure once symptoms show. Any warm-blooded animal can be infected after being bitten by a rabies-infected animal. In Europe, foxes are the most common victims, but domestic animals such as dogs, cats and cattle also catch rabies.

When you are in countries where rabies occurs, keep well away from stray dogs and cats even if they appear docile. Mostly, a rabid dog will appear withdrawn, and not show any obvious symptoms, but it may become very aggressive and attack without warning; cats may also attack and bite. Don't touch any dead animals.

If you are bitten by any dog in a country where rabies occurs, first wash the bite thoroughly with soap and water (detergent actually kills the rabies virus). Then see a doctor as soon as possible. Try to remember what the dog looked like and where the incident occurred so the animal can be caught and examined. Rabies does not occur in Britain at the present time.

Book list

The Spur Book of Map & Compass. Brown & Hunter (Spur).
The Walker's Handbook. Hugh Westacott (Penguin).
Reader's Digest Guide to Bicycle Repairs. (Reader's Digest).
The Piccolo Bicycle Book. Richard Ballantine (Piccolo).
Spotter's Guide to The Weather. Wilson and Mansfield (Usborne).
Better Camping. Alan Ryalls & Roger Marchant (Kaye & Ward).
Camping for Young People. Anthony Greenbank (Piccolo).
The Scout Standard and *The Advanced Scout Standard.* Steve Scholes (The Scout Association).

Enjoy Camping. Doug Mountford (The Scout Association).
First Aid Manual. The authorized manual of the British Red Cross Society, St John Ambulance and St Andrew's Ambulance Association.
The British Red Cross Society Practical First Aid Manual. (E.P. Publishing).
Modern First Aid. A.S. Playfair (Hamlyn).
First Aid for Hill Walkers and Climbers. Jane Renout and Stewart Hulse (Penguin).
Life Saving and Water Safety. (The Royal Life Saving Society).

Useful addresses

The Royal Society for Prevention of Accidents (RoSPA), Cannon House, The Priory, Queensway, Birmingham. RoSPA organize cycling proficiency tests.
Youth Hostels Association, Trevelyan House, St Stephen's Hill, St Alban's, Hertfordshire.
The Girl Guides Association, 17-19 Buckingham Palace Road, London SW1.
The Scout Association, Baden-Powell House, Queen's Gate, London SW7.

The Camping Club of Great Britain and Ireland, 11 Grosvenor Place, London SW1. The club has a Camping Club Youth section.
British Red Cross Society, 9 Grosvenor Crescent, London SW1. Runs accident prevention and first aid courses.
St John Ambulance Association 29 Weymouth Street, London W1.
Royal Life Saving Society, 14 Devonshire Street, Portland Place, London W1. Runs courses in life saving and water safety.

Answers ... page 25

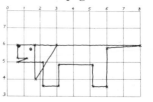

... page 27

The shortest route by road between Abbey Top and Dry Gulch is 5.7 kilometres. The shortest walking route is 3.8 kilometres; follow the road to Leadown, then the footpath to Dry Gulch.

Index